PREACHING WITH INTEGRITY

Kenton C. Anderson

Kregel
Academic & Professional

Preaching with Integrity

Published by Kregel Publications, a division of Kregel, Inc., P.O. Box 2607, Grand Rapids, MI 49501. Kregel Publications provides trusted, biblical publications for Christian growth and service. Your comments and suggestions are valued.

Library of Congress Cataloging-in-Publication Data
Anderson, Kenton C.
Preaching with integrity / by Kenton C. Anderson.
    p. cm.
Includes bibliographical references.
1. Preaching. I. Title.
BV4211.3.A54   2003   251—dc22   2003015991

ISBN 0-8254-2021-0

Printed in the United States of America

1 2 3 4 5 / 07 06 05 04 03

PREACHING
WITH
INTEGRITY

Other books in the *Preaching With Series:*

To my family—
my wife, Karen, and my three children,
Kelsey, Kirk, and Katelyn—
for whose sake I choose to
live with integrity.

Contents

Foreword

Is it possible that—to the ears of those under 40—your preaching sounds as dated as a sermon by Jonathan Edwards?

Some things about the ministry of the Word never change. The good news of salvation through Christ, the truths about who God is and what he has done, the doctrines held in trust for centuries by the church—all are timeless.

But other things about the ministry of the Word will never stop changing: our hearers, our culture, the dress of thought and language, and the questions posed today. The sermons of Edwards and Spurgeon remind us that preaching never stands still.

Preaching with Integrity focuses on how preaching that stands firmly on the full authority of Scripture—and the need to proclaim its verbal absolutes—can at the same time adapt to reach a generation tuned to story and feelings.

In many ways the divine, unchanging side of preaching is easier to understand than the human side. How does God work through the humanity of preachers? How do we preach in a way that takes into full account the humanity of our hearers?

From beginning to end I found helpful, satisfying answers in this book.

As I neared the end, I was reminded that what *Preaching with Integrity* models—the power of story—is real. In the climactic scene (Anderson embeds the principles of preaching in a fictional story), I found myself with a lump in my throat. Frankly, I was surprised by my reaction. I knew I was reading fiction. I have read a great deal about story writing and have written about it myself, so you would think that knowing the techniques of story, I would be less susceptible to its emotional power. Not so.

Kent Anderson shows how we can wed the moving elements of story with our responsibility to proclaim and lay bare the Scriptures. Give it a try.

—Craig Brian Larson
Editor of preaching resources, PreachingToday.com
Christianity Today International

Preface

I began writing this book about one year after completing my first book, *Preaching with Conviction*. Having written that book in narrative form, I thought I would write this in a more traditional form, in part to avoid being typecast. I wanted to show I am capable of writing a conventional book. My wife, however, was less than enthusiastic. "Oh, you want to write a boring book," she said.

I shared this with my publisher, Dennis Hillman, who said, "No, please don't write a boring book." He said, "You could really help pastors by writing a narrative that deals with the struggle preachers have with temptation." As Dennis described pain felt by pastors he has known, I thought of those within my own sphere of concern who struggle with integrity.

I began to wonder what it would be like if we were to meet with Pastor Jack Newman, the fictional pastor of *Preaching with Conviction*, one year after that mystery was solved. I wondered what might happen if he found himself in a situation that would test his personal credibility. None of us is above temptation. We all have our limits. The question is, how will we respond when we bump into the boundaries? This book explores these issues.

In the midst of this exploration, we will take a second look at the Integrative Preaching model that was described in *Preaching with Conviction*. Instead of tracking the model by a developmental process, as in the first book, this time I structure the book around the sermon model. After finishing the narrative and sermon clinic at the end of the book, the reader should have a reasonably solid grasp of the integrative sermon.

I'm indebted to a group of my students who read the first draft and offered encouragement and helpful criticism. David Chow, Brent Friesen, Jim Nightingale, and Brad Naylor are the kind of students that motivate a professor.

I also found impetus from an array of pastors and preachers who read *Conviction* and took time to e-mail me or contact me from every corner of the world. These preachers described ways in which God is using these stories and ideas to build his kingdom and encourage its leaders. I've been allowed to mentor a group of leaders in Belfast, an emerging preaching movement in the Netherlands, a group of U.S. Army chaplains in Texas, and other groups in Seoul, Korea, and in South America. I have had contact with many others who live across the United States and Canada. I'm both humbled and emboldened by this knowledge. I hope readers of this volume, too, will let me know how God uses these ideas in their lives and ministries.

You may notice that I haven't cluttered up the story with lots of footnotes and citations. The bibliography of resources used in my extensive research is available. Check the "Reviews" page on my Web site, www.preaching.org. There are limitations inherent in the narrative form of this book. I offer a more systematic and complete approach in two teaching sections at the back. One of these sections is set up as a clinic in integrative preaching, while the other offers some introductory thoughts toward a homiletic anthropology.

I'm aware that this way of approaching the topic is different. I came to know how unusual it is when *Preaching with Conviction* was shortlisted for a book award granted to Canadian Christians in print. I didn't win, which may have had something to do with the fact that the book was entered in the "novel" category. That put it up against Janette Oke and other such masters of Christian fiction. I'm sure the novelists were surprised to discover that they were up against a book on homiletics.

The characterizations in the book are, of course, fictional but the issues are not. People still need to hear from God. You'll help them as you offer them the Bible. When the world changes and the ground shakes, the Word of the Lord stands forever.

PART 1

Narrative

1

Fault Lines

TELL THE STORY

At first he thought it was a train. Living near the tracks, Jack Newman was accustomed to feeling the foundation quiver whenever heavily loaded rail cars rolled by his back yard. He often wondered how his home held together, given all the jarring.

But this was no train. That became obvious as he watched the curtains dance, the books on his shelf tumble, and the hallway mirror come crashing to the floor. This was an earthquake. Not a big one, mind you. The mirror had always been a little "wonky." It was one of those things he'd never gotten around to fixing. Too late now.

It was over as soon as it started. The damage was minor. The house settled back into its accustomed fixedness. Nothing to worry about. No harm done.

So why did it leave him feeling so unsettled? Why the uneasy feeling in his stomach? It had been some time since Jack had felt this way. He didn't like it.

The letter felt like dead weight in Henry Ellis's hand. Signed, sealed, yet he would give almost anything not to have to deliver it. Not that anybody would be shocked. Things like this happened, he told himself. Well, maybe they hadn't happened in the past, but they did today, and people would understand. They'd have to understand.

The pressure—everyone knew the pressure on pastors. People would be a lot more forgiving these days.

Henry almost believed himself.

He hurt as if *he* had something to confess. Somehow he wished he could have. A letter carrying his own confession would have been less traumatic. Certainly the pain didn't feel any less for his personal innocence. When you love the one who hurts, *you* hurt. You cry late at night when you think no one else can hear. Or you lie awake and listen to the sobbing of your wife. Disappointed tears. Tears of broken promises and shame. It was hard to hear her crying.

Henry wasn't ashamed. It surprised him that he wasn't. He ought to have been ashamed, he was quite sure. Instead, he felt a pure pain, unalloyed by the guilt of misplaced pride. He hurt because his son hurt. That was all.

That was enough.

Tom Newman jumped in his car even before he knew where he was going. He'd been in the editing room checking tape when the tremors hit. Wrapped up in his work, he might not have noticed the vibrations, except that his glass of water had fallen over, dampening his first-draft script for the evening telecast. No matter. It wasn't much of a newscast anyway. He'd been waiting for something to happen, something fresh, something dramatic. Here was a breaking story. There had to be some way he could spin it.

People wanted information. They turned on their radios or picked up a newspaper. Increasingly they turned to their Internet browsers. Mostly, though, they still turned on their TV. Newman didn't have that luxury, however. Tom *was* TV.

Backing out of his parking space he hit his cell phone speed dial. "Where is it?" he barked.

Terri Jones was used to Tom's abruptness. She loved the news business as much as he did. The adrenaline kick was addictive. "Not sure yet." She was dialing through the squawk of her police band radio. "Hold on. Might be something. . . ."

"Come on, Terri. Am I going right or going left? You want me downtown or in the valley? There's got to be something . . ."

"Okay, downtown. There's a call. . . . What did you say? I can't re . . ." The news anchor's assistant made no attempt to hide her impatience. "Okay, Tom, forget downtown. We've had at least two calls from the airport. Something about cracks in the runway. It might be nothing, but maybe you can do something with it."

Before the sentence was complete, Tom had pulled hard on the wheel of his Beemer. U-turns weren't permitted on this stretch of the highway. A siren would be helpful, Tom thought—maybe some of those flashing blue and red lights hidden behind the front grill. Tom wasn't afraid to assert the privileges normally reserved for police cruisers and ambulances. He was in the service of the people's right to know, and these days, people wanted to know quickly.

Sure, he could make it into something. He wasn't afraid to manipulate the data, if it came to that. That was how the job worked. He had thirty minutes to fill every evening. It didn't matter if World War III was breaking out, he had the same thirty minutes to fill as he did when the biggest piece of news was an unexpected cold front that imperiled tomato plants. It wasn't that he stretched the news. It was just that some days were thinner than others.

It had been a thin week, and clearly this wasn't much of an earthquake. But maybe he'd be lucky. Maybe planes would be delayed because of problems with the runway. Stories of stranded airport passengers always played well.

—⊷⊶—

Pastor Jack Newman didn't see the letter right away. It was on his desk where Henry had placed it not more than twenty minutes earlier, buried under a pile of notes, magazines, and junk mail that Jack had pulled from his briefcase and tossed onto his desk to deal with later.

He allowed himself a moment—a good moment. He was content, and it felt good to be content. The last year had been peaceful. No, it had been better than that. Ever since that incident with Philip Andrews, Jack had felt renewed in his ministry.[1] His preaching had been his particular passion in recent months. He was still no Billy Graham—no crowds of penitents streamed forward as he concluded. But people were responding, one at a time, like ordinary people did. They were interested in the message. They were interested in the Bible, and that was something Jack had thought might never be the case again.

He'd misjudged the power of solid biblical preaching. Now he knew that exposition was no relic of a bygone era. God still spoke when his Word was preached. He'd seen the changed lives, and not just in Philip Andrews, although the change in that man continued to surprise him. But he'd also seen newness in the lives of people he counseled. He'd seen it in young people who no longer treated him like he was irrelevant. Mostly he saw it in a renewed attention that sparked in the eyes of his congregation when he preached.

Perhaps the greatest thing was the change he felt in himself. Now he felt invested in the sermon. No longer was it a pastoral requirement he had to force himself to attend to every week, whether he had anything to say or not. Now he was encouraged that the sermon felt like the high point of his weekly ministry. It was his opportunity to help people hear from God.

His moment of reflection over, Jack set about his work. He liked to clear his mail before he got going on his sermon. He was always one to eat his vegetables separate from the meat and both separate from the potatoes. He would never be one of those people who could listen to music, watch television, read a book, and offer quality time to his wife, all at the same time. What did they call that kind of thing? *Multitasking*—probably it was just a cover that allowed people with weak attention spans to overwhelm themselves with stimuli.

There was a lot of mail. Some of it even looked interesting. Henry

Ellis's letter caught his attention right away. The handwritten address and uncanceled postage stamp stood out against the bulk mail and junk mail in the pile. Jack puzzled over it. Why did Henry need to write a letter? He came by the church two or three times a week.

There could have been any number of reasons, Jack realized—a party invitation, a note of encouragement. Either would have been consistent with Henry's character. Somehow, Jack doubted it. This had the feel of bad news. He could sense it in his pastor's gut.

Dear Pastor, . . .

Too formal, Jack complained to himself. Not a good start.

I'm not sure why I'm writing this. I could have just as easily come by and told you to your face.

Henry's handwriting was wobbly. Jack wasn't sure if it betrayed a weak heart or just a wobbly wrist.

It's not that I'm unsure of your reaction. I'm very sure of it, and I guess I'd just prefer not to have to deal with it, at least not yet. There'll be time enough for us to talk, I'm sure.

Jack was starting to feel lumpy in his throat.

It's about Chris.

Jack's heart did a double beat. Chris Ellis was Henry's son and Jack Newman's best friend. They lived too far apart to spend much time together anymore. Chris and Jack had been college roommates some twenty-five years ago. They'd connected in the way young men sometimes do. They liked the same sports and the same girls. They shared a sense of calling. When it came time to graduate from seminary, both had a full-time ministry opportunity within a week, on opposite sides of the same city.

The distance was just enough to make it hard to maintain their relationship. Once or twice a year they found themselves together at an event of one kind or another. They'd make plans to get together—perhaps a barbecue, or maybe they'd go out to eat. There were conventions, of course, and pastors' conferences. But Jack realized that it had been a year and a half since they'd last laid eyes on one another.

. . . I know how much you and Chris cared about each other, Henry continued. *And I wanted you to hear it from me before you heard it from somebody else.*

Jack felt his heart tremor. Things like this aren't supposed to be shocking anymore, not with sexual failures by clergy spread across the news. Pastors fall. It happens. Gone is the mystique of the position. Pastors aren't so holy as to avoid the allure of a wily woman, or even a woman who isn't so much "wily" as troubled. Most of these situations involved an ordinary, vulnerable woman—and an ordinary, vulnerable man, Jack reminded himself.

But not Chris!

Chris has checked into the Monarch Hotel, Henry concluded.

He'll be keeping out of sight, but he might like a visit with you. *Maybe you could encourage him.*

Anger now.

Chris—you . . . you . . . idiot! The word wasn't strong enough, but his pastor's vocabulary didn't allow for the words that would have felt appropriate. What's wrong with you?

The words burst out and reverberated around the bookshelves: "What were you thinking?"

What about Chloe? Jack admired Chloe. She had a strong personality and didn't put up with a lot of nonsense. Her good sense had guided Chris through a lot of the garbage that pastors face. He pictured her now, tear-stained and probably very angry. Whatever would happen to Chloe . . . and to Chris . . . and to his ministry?

—◦◦◦◦—

Tom Newman wasn't sure what he'd expected. He knew this wasn't going to be the San Andreas Fault, but somehow he thought it would be a little more dramatic than this. The airport runway was barely cracked, with a thin, jagged, break across the concrete. The crack was less than an inch wide. It hardly seemed significant, though apparently the Airport Authority felt differently. The runway had been closed until it could be examined more carefully.

That wasn't Tom's problem. He needed to make a crater out of a crack. He wasn't even sure the fissure would be visible on TV. He framed the potential TV scene with his hands. It wasn't very promising—not enough drama. "Any chance we could get some emergency barricade sawhorses or something that would make this look like something has actually happened here?"

Bob Wilson, Tom's cameraman and sidekick, gave him a knowing wink. He had a good eye for these situations. A few orange cones and several dozen feet of fluorescent yellow tape, and before you know it you've got a disaster scene. "I'm going to see if we can get one of those baggage carts moved over here—the ones with the flashing lights," he said. "We'll position the light so it strobes into the camera. If we hit it just at dusk it'll give us the effect we need."

Fifteen minutes later, telejournalist Tom Newman, his hair combed and his tie straight, stood in front of the cameras as part of a scene that looked to the viewers like the site of a major catastrophe. "Airport officials are unable to tell us when the runway will reopen," Tom warned the audience.

"We've got to ensure the safety of the traveling public," an official-looking baggage handler said, gazing seriously into the camera.

It wasn't one of Tom Newman's proudest moments. Funny how these things were bothering him these days. He wanted to tell himself he was doing a public service, but he knew better. He was creating a story. These kinds of minor tremors happen all the time along the coast. There'd be another one in a few months, and maybe some day something big would come along. It would not come in time for tonight's newscast, however, and probably not tomorrow's. He shook his head hard as if to clear the unpleasantness.

"Did I do all right?" the handler asked. He had a baggage tag and a pen in his hand. He seemed to be hoping for an autograph.

"You did fine," Tom said, signing his name with disinterest.

People will be scared to travel now for weeks, he said to himself as he abandoned the scene.

Jack Newman entered the offices of his denomination's ministry center. He turned left when he should have turned right. Apparently they'd remodeled since he'd last been there. Jack wasn't a strong denominational guy. Not that he had any particular argument about his group of churches.

He'd just never paid much attention. In this, he wasn't much different than most of the pastors of his age group. The denomination just didn't seem relevant to the day-to-day operation of his ministry. He'd never found the office particularly useful to his needs. Deep down maybe he even questioned how much they understood contemporary ministry. In truth, he had not really given it much thought until now.

Chris was ordained by the same denomination, though his church was in an adjacent district. Maybe Stewart Rylie could give Jack some insight into the nature of the problem generally, if not into the particulars of Chris's situation.

"Jack!" Stewart said in greeting. "Glad to see you still know the way over here." There was no malice in his tone; no subtlety either.

"Think of it as a good thing," Jack responded, surprised by the warmth he felt toward his district supervisor. "I've been doing my job and you haven't needed to pay me any attention." He meant it as humor, but it didn't really come off. Stewart was kind enough to chuckle.

"We do more around here than rescue sinking pastors."

Jack didn't respond to that one. It was true that the ministry center sponsored any number of positive initiatives to encourage church health and growth, but the truth was that Rylie spent more time putting out fires than the fire department. That, of course, was why Jack had come.

"Have you got anything other than coffee in this place?" Jack asked.

"Sure we do. The fridge is in the corner. It's pretty well stocked."

Jack found a cola brand he liked hiding behind someone's bag lunch. He followed Rylie into a cozy office and eased himself into a deep-cushioned armchair.

"I wanted to talk to you about Chris Ellis." Jack got right to the point. He didn't know how else to start.

"I wondered," Rylie said.

"Tell me I've got it wrong, Stew," Jack pleaded. "Tell me there are extenuating circumstances—something that could help me understand. 'Cause the way it is, this just hurts too much."

"Have you talked to him yet?"

"No." Jack paused. "I don't know what I'm going to say. I don't know what I'll do. I just might punch him in the face."

"Natural enough reaction," Rylie said quietly. "You guys were close, as I recall, . . . since seminary?"

"College. . . . You know, Chris's father, Henry, is in my congregation. He couldn't even tell me to my face. He had to put it in a letter."

"He'll talk to you when he's ready."

Jack rested his face in his hands. He wasn't crying. Perhaps he was too angry for tears.

"What can you tell me, Stew?"

"Not much that wouldn't violate confidence, I'm afraid."

The room fell silent for a time. Stewart Rylie knew his business. He wasn't one to push things prematurely. Jack Newman fidgeted. A couple of times he began to say something before aborting the attempt. He rose from his seat and walked over to the window without bothering to look out.

"This stuff happens, Jack," Stewart said.

"How does it happen?"

"Pastors are weak. You know that. I know a lot of people don't think so. People are still dealing with a romanticized sense of the perfect pastor who's supposed to be above every temptation and beyond every natural human impulse. For the most part, we like it that way. Preachers get addicted to the praise of the people and that's a dangerous place to be. Inevitably the pressure builds. We find we can't even live up to the expectations we've placed on ourselves. We start to experience stress and that puts us in a vulnerable spot."

"You never see it coming," Jack reflected.

"You never see *her* coming," Stewart said. "It's rarely someone you'd expect. We have an idea of this incredibly beautiful temptress with a knockout body and an experienced air. But that would be too easy. We know enough to engage our defenses against the obvious temptation. Usually, it's someone more ordinary, a housewife or a counseling client. Many times they're as surprised by the sudden feelings as the pastor is. They're vulnerable. They're hurting. Often, they are not all that well put together emotionally. They see the pastor as a source of strength. It may be that he's the only sympathetic male she's met. He doesn't have to be good looking or wealthy, or even wise. He just has to be there with a smile on his face and an understanding spirit."

"Is that what happened to Chris?" Jack interrupted.

"Something like that," Rylie responded. "Chris reacted the way a lot of pastors do under pressure. He enjoyed the attention, more than he realized. He found himself attracted to her weakness. He didn't discern his own weakness until he was in too deep. He'd committed himself, emotionally at least. He liked it. I'm not sure he liked her, but he liked the way she made him feel. Risk. Romance. It's intoxicating."

Jack was listening, though not with any sense of comfort. "How often does this happen?" he eventually asked.

"You want the statistics?" Stewart asked.

"Sure. Statistics—anything to give me an idea what I'm up against."

"There are various studies. Generally, the numbers suggest that 10 percent of clergy are guilty of sexual misconduct, and another 15 percent have come close to the line."

"That's one in four when you add it up," Jack protested.

"That's right," Stewart confirmed. "Roman Catholics have already lost one quarter of their active priests due to sexual and marital reasons, and Protestants aren't far behind. One denominational study reported that clergy sexually exploit parishioners twice as often as do sexual therapists."[2]

"But that's just wrong," Jack protested. "That can't possibly be correct. Surely, we ought to be . . ."

Rylie rose abruptly and crossed to his filing cabinet. He pulled out a few folders and examined the contents, eventually settling on one. "Let me quote the research to you, Jack: 'Present research indicates the incidence of sexual abuse by clergy has reached horrific proportions. Two seminal studies in 1984 reported 12 and 12.7 percent of ministers had engaged in sexual intercourse with members, and 37 and 39 percent acknowledged sexually inappropriate behavior."

Jack looked like he wanted to argue.

"You want the footnotes?" Rylie asked.

Jack slumped back; 1984 was a long time ago. It could only have gotten worse. He wondered just how much worse. He remembered back to those days. He read about this kind of thing, but it had seemed distant, reserved for other churches in less faithful denominations.

He'd thought of it as a natural consequence of a slackened commit-ment to the Scriptures. But now, this kind of pastoral promiscuity was evident all around him.

"More recent statistics suggest that 64 percent of pastors and church staff struggle with sexual addiction or compulsion," Stewart Rylie continued. "Twenty-five percent have admitted to having sexual in-tercourse with someone besides their wife while married, after they'd accepted Christ. Another 14 percent admitted some form of sexual contact short of intercourse. Those numbers were published in 1999."[3]

Pastoral Infidelity

▶ 64 percent of pastors confess to a sexual addiction.

▶ 25 percent of pastors confess to having sexual intercourse with someone other than their wives while married, and since they were converted to Jesus Christ.

▶ 14 percent of pastors confess to having sexual contact with a parishioner short of sexual intercourse.

Jack looked into Stewart Rylie's eyes without comprehension. These figures were staggering. They were horrific . . . obscene.

"Do you want more?" Rylie asked.

Jack didn't want any more numbers. "We ought to be able to do better than this, Stewart," he said, his anger coming to the surface. "We're preachers, right? We stand in front of the people week after week and offer them the very Word of God. We speak as the spokes-men of God Himself. We can't be doing this kind of thing. We can't afford this kind of foolishness."

"I'm with you, Jack."

"I mean, I get it," Jack continued. "I understand that we're weak. I get that we're frail. But when I stand in the pulpit, I forfeit the right to give in to that kind of weakness. I'm there to speak the words of God as if from the very mouth of God. I can't have people wondering about my sincerity. It's not just my credibility on the line. The credi-bility of the gospel is at risk."

"Well, . . ." Rylie was about to say something about how the gospel is bigger than any human sin. He was going to say something about the mystery of God's willingness to use flawed humans to proclaim great glories, but Jack wasn't listening at the moment.

"Don't these people know that every time one of *them* steps out of line, every one of *us* gets hit with the same stereotype—and what a stereotype. It's repulsive! It was bad enough when pastors were thought of as kindly old gentlemen who were occasionally helpful but mostly irrelevant. Now, if they think of us at all, people get a picture of a hypocritical sexual predator. It makes me want to . . ."

Stewart thought he'd better let Jack take his rant to its end. Except that was the end. Jack collapsed into his chair. With no more frenzy, he was free to feel the impact. Tears collected around his eyelids.

"Are you afraid, Jack?" The district minister paused long before he said it. He'd seen this look before.

Jack wasn't quick to answer. Then the word came out with a physical shudder. "Yes."

"What are you afraid of, Jack?"

Longer pause.

"Jack?"

"I'm afraid I'll end up like Chris."

Was he? Was he really afraid he'd fall? He'd never given it a moment's worry in the past. He had a strong marriage—a strong faith. There wasn't any fear that he'd throw it all away. Things could never get as bad as all that, could they?

It wasn't far from the ministry center to Henry's house, so Jack deliberately turned in the wrong direction. He wasn't ready to meet Henry quite yet. He needed more time, but he knew he couldn't go back to the office. He had to attend to business, but maybe not just yet. He'd take the long way—drive around a little first—collect some courage.

Looking for a distraction, Jack turned the radio on. The call-in show's host was talking about the recent earthquake, if you could call it that. The mild tremor was predictable. Every time there was a little shake the radio station trotted out whatever seismic experts they could find—anyone who could sound authoritative. The media provided a crash course in the movement of geological plates. It would all be forgotten in a month.

Jack had experienced an earthquake, but it had nothing to do with seismology.

Pastor Jack pulled his car tight to the curb in front of Henry's familiar light yellow home. The house was always so inviting. Now that Henry and Anna were retired, they'd been able to give time to their gardens and lawns. Tending flowers was a lot less demanding than tending people, though ultimately not so rewarding.

The curtains and blinds were open. Nothing indicated the pain inside. Jack whispered a prayer before shutting off the engine. It was a little flat as prayers go, but it seemed the right thing to do.

Henry Ellis welcomed his pastor warmly. There was a rich smile on his face, no sign of the tears Jack knew he must have shed. Anna looked depleted. She smiled wanly but clearly she wasn't up to entertaining. Jack wasn't sure he'd ever seen her without makeup before. Her age was evident.

"I'll be out back, Henry," she said. "It is nice to see you, Jack. Thank you for caring." She smiled again, this time from her heart.

"I'll . . . "

He was going to finish with "pray for you," but it sounded lame, so he choked off the words before expressing them. He would pray for them, and he really did believe prayer would make a difference. But saying it sounded so cliché. *The words slide off the tongue too easily.* So Jack stood there, trying to look sincere.

"I know," Anna said. She left the room gracefully and graciously.

"Sit down," Henry said. "Here, this is the best chair in the house. It's yours whenever you come here."

"You're too kind, Henry," Jack said. He meant it. *Henry's world has just been shaken, and he's trying to make me feel comfortable. Maybe it's just his habit. Maybe it's just the kind of man Henry Ellis is. You learn a lot about a person when he's tested.*

"How are you doing, Jack?" Henry was all sincerity.

"Worse than you, by the look of it," Jack responded.

"I'm a great actor," Henry said.

"It hurts," Jack said.

"It hurts bad," Henry agreed.

The two lapsed into silence. It was a comfortable silence. The clock on the mantle announced its presence with an antique chime.

"What are we going to do, Jack?"

"I'm going to go talk to him."

"Good. He'll like that."

"Are you sure? I'm not sure how anxious I'd be to welcome friends at a time like this." In truth, Jack was very sure. He wouldn't want any part of anyone coming to his aid. He'd go underground—missing in action.

"He'll be embarrassed, and he ought to be. But he knows a friend when he sees one, and if ever he needed a friend, it's now."

"I don't know how much help I'll be," Jack said. "I just don't know what to say. I don't know how this kind of thing happens. I don't know how to help."

"You'll know what to do," Henry said. "It will come from your heart and from the Holy Spirit. When you really love somebody, it shows, and that's what he needs."

Jack accepted the truth of the statement, though he couldn't yet perceive the application.

"I've come to realize that it's frightening."

"What are you frightened of?" Henry asked.

"I've never really believed that something like this could happen to me or to people close to me," Jack said. "I've always believed it to be fairly simple. As long as I take care of myself spiritually, emotionally, and physically, I'd be all right."

Henry shifted in his chair, showing interest.

Jack was thinking about what he was going to say. "Maybe I felt that if I thought about the possibility of moral failure, I was somehow inviting it. Or maybe I was just too simpleminded. You know, I've got a job to do, so I just go out and do it. I don't think about what would happen if I got stupid. I don't think of myself in those terms. I don't consider myself to be stupid."

"You're not stupid," Henry confirmed. It was an obvious comment, but Jack felt better hearing it.

"I remember reading an article several years ago, written by Bill Hybels. He suggested that we should keep watch over our lives by visualizing a dashboard with three concerns measured by gauges. One gauge measures our spiritual life, one our emotional life, and one our physical life. If any of them start to read low, it's time to pull over and fill up."[4]

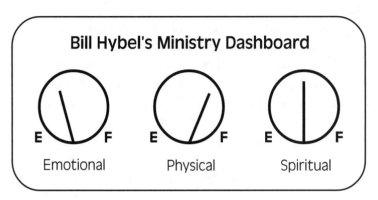

"Good advice," Henry said. "It's been more intuitive than intentional with me, but I've taken the same approach over the years. You always want to maintain an appropriate base level of spiritual nourishment and physical fitness, but there have been times when I've felt particularly depleted, so I'd take a day out to be alone with God in his Word."

"I've found a long afternoon nap can work wonders," Jack admitted.

"Just make sure the congregation doesn't hear about that one," Henry said. "Tough to justify siestas to the board."

Jack grinned at Henry, then choked it off. He didn't want to feel like grinning.

"I doubt it was that simple for Chris," Henry said. "No doubt he was under pressure. Clearly, he wasn't acting rationally. He had too much to lose. I guess we should never underestimate our ability to lie to ourselves. Sin is so deceitful."

"*Sin.*" Having named the problem, Henry had little left to say. He smiled awkwardly and left the room without comment.

Tell the Story . . .

Fiedler Park was a half block from Henry's house. Jack decided to pay a visit. With a cell phone and a laptop he could set up a virtual office at one of the picnic benches overlooking the river. It was one of his favorite places. Many of Jack's best sermons had been prayed over and talked through on the pathways along the river.

He opened his briefcase and pulled out his sermon file for this Sunday. The sermon already was well developed. Recently, Jack had disciplined himself to work further in advance in his preaching. He found that by working on two or three sermons at once, he could buy himself more time for his sermons to develop. It was like cooking a sermon in a slow cooker instead of a microwave. Slow cooking his sermons made for a deeper, more nourishing meal.

	Slow Cooking Sermons		
	Week 1	Week 2	Week 3
Discovery	Sermon C	Sermon D	Sermon E
Construction	Sermon B	Sermon C	Sermon D
Assimilation	Sermon A	Sermon B	Sermon C

The beauty of his plan was that he was still able to put the same number of hours into sermon preparation as he ever had, but because the process was spread over a longer preparation period there was more opportunity for God to teach him the truth of his text.

Each week he worked on three different sermons at the same time. On one he'd do *discovery,* looking to understand the *message* he'd preach two weeks later. He'd also find time to *construct* a second sermon, building on work he'd begun the week before. On a third sermon he'd do what he called *assimilation,* preparing and applying the sermon he'd begun work on two weeks earlier. This was the sermon he was about to deliver.

Jack had that work before him now. He liked to be ready well in advance of Sunday—no late Saturday nights, cramming for the sermon in the morning. He loved to assimilate his sermons so that they were part of his nature—so that they lived and breathed inside of him. He liked to live with the sermon, working out the implications in his own life even as he grew comfortable with the words and the propositions.

He prayed over the sermon, deliberately putting time into his schedule to pray over the words he'd preach. He wanted to be full of the sermon so the truth and impact would flow over and out to the people before him on Sunday. It was good to be intentional about such a thing. He didn't assume he was ready to preach just because he had an outline. He needed to meet with God. He knew from hard experience that it wouldn't happen if he didn't intend it.

He opened the file and began to sort through the pages, computer printouts of his text in various versions, overwritten with his barely legible scribble, multicolored highlights, circles, and underlines. Interleaved were scraps of yellow legal-size paper covered with ideas, thoughts, questions, diagrams, and possibilities and sections of photocopied commentaries, atlases, and Bible encyclopedia. The first page in the file, however, featured the fruit of all Jack's labor. On that page was a circle intersected by two lines. These lines divided the circle into four quadrants. Quadrants were neatly labeled: (1) "What's the story?" (2) "What's the point?" (3) "What's the problem?" and (4) "What's the difference?" Within the quadrants, Jack had arranged the elements of his sermon. It still surprised him just how much that little diagram had helped his preaching since that eventful week a year or so ago.

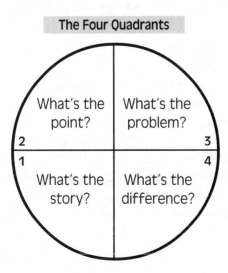

The Four Quadrants

Jack felt his heart flutter as he looked at the words on the page. The text described the *unshakeable* kingdom of God—earthquake language. It was uncanny.

Theologically, he was committed to the idea that preaching was helping people hear from God. Already, he knew God's voice would be heard more loudly this Sunday, if for no other reason than that the earth had rumbled. Some Sundays he had to work harder to connect people to a text. It wouldn't be a problem this time. His sermon would be like an episode of *Law and Order*—"ripped from the headlines."

He'd chosen to speak from Hebrews 12:28–29, a passage that described the Christian's connection with God's kingdom and the kind of worship that ought to result in response to God's great gift. But it was the context that had Jack's attention, the imagery, the *backstory*.

Jack had trained himself to begin with the question, "What's the story?" It was his way of getting in touch with the human context of the passage. Every text has a story about real humans with real lives dealing with real problems and real predicaments. He'd found that if he could help his listeners understand the original real-life story embedded in the text, they'd be prepared to listen more readily.

Biblical texts, he knew, describe actual historical situations. While those ancient situations are distant from contemporary life in some respects, the two horizons of past and present have the common denominator of basic humanity. Hermeneutics textbooks can make a big deal about the gap between the ancient and the contemporary. Jack felt that this distance is overplayed. What is the text about? People! People aren't so different today. Jack's job was to help his listeners appreciate these ancient people's stories.

In fact, Jack knew, every sermon should relate three stories: the original story (their story); the listener's story (our story); and the bigger story of what God is doing across time (his story). The preaching challenge is to find a way to integrate these three stories so listeners recognize *our story* in *their story*. Usually, this was achieved through understanding *his story*—what God was and is doing. Integrating the three stories connects the contemporary to the ancient in a message that rings with relevance.

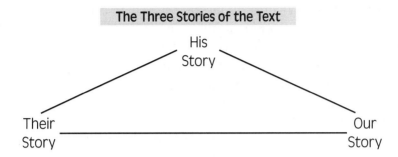

The Three Stories of the Text

His
Story

Their
Story

Our
Story

Hebrews 12:28–29 directs a Jewish New Testament audience to reflect deeply on their earlier corporate history. These people had long memories. When the writer of the letter to the Hebrews spoke of being careful about touching mountains that burned with fire because of the earth-shaking voice of God, their memory immediately shifted to Mount Sinai. In Exodus 19, Moses met with God on the mountain while the people gathered below. Verse 18 of Exodus 19 says that Mount Sinai was covered with smoke as the Lord descended in fire. Smoke billowed up and the whole mountain shook violently as God made his voice heard.

The potent memory reminded first-century Jewish Christians of the God who could bring the earth to nothing, simply by the sound of his voice. Don't refuse the One who speaks, the text said (Heb. 12:25). If they didn't escape back then when God warned them on earth, how much less a chance do we have today, when God warns us from heaven? This is not a subtle warning. Back then, the letter said, God shook the earth with his voice. This time he would shake both the earth and the heavens (v. 26). This message from God is cataclysmic—a wholesale upheaval of the cosmos, the universe entire turned upside-down and shaken hard by the voice of Almighty God.

Judgment!

All this talk about earthquakes was a little unsettling when one had just felt the tremors—literally. Jack knew that Richter rumblings and seismic shaking portended more than the shifting of underground plates. Both the movements of San Andreas and the travails of Tsunami were part of the groaning of creation under its bondage to decay

(Rom. 8:19–21), all part of the present period of in-between. The creation and all who live within it trudge on between the first and second comings, waiting patiently (or less so) for the day when all is restored and the sons of God are revealed. Until that day we struggle. The earth shudders and the people cringe under the weight of a world gone awry. People fall and people fail as the world tumbles on. People like Chris Ellis. People like Jack Newman.

A bird bolder than others of its kind landed on the bench, startling Jack out of his thoughts. Almost as soon as it touched down, it took flight again, only to stop on the next bench over. Jack watched as the bird continued the pattern, a series of short-haul flights like a plane flying the "milk run" for a cut-rate airline. He returned his attention to his work.

"I'm going to want to tell the story," Jack told himself. Texts like this are difficult in that they don't offer a clear narrative. On the other hand, the human issues are clear enough. It isn't hard to understand the fear of judgment. Jack would have to fill out the story with contemporary material, which wouldn't be difficult. The story is all around him, people struggling under the threat of judgment, trying to find footing as they walk along the fault lines. Sometimes the ground shakes, the culture shifts, and the people stumble. He was all too familiar with the pattern.

Tell the Story

Engaging people by connecting them
to the human story in the text.

▶ Identify the three stories of the sermon: their story, our story, and his story.
▶ Arrange the plot elements, setting, characters, problem, climax, . . .
▶ Identify the sensual elements of the sermon, what it smells like, looks like, tastes like, . . .

Jack scrolled through his recent memory, recalling the experiences of the people in his congregation—people who'd lost jobs and loved ones. He thought about Martha Frederickson. Martha had two teen-age daughters, no husband, and a malignancy in her breast. Just two months ago the doctor had shaken her world with the news. Maybe he could tell her story, Jack thought. He could talk about the anxiety, the uncertainty Martha felt.

He could describe the evening spent in the Frederickson living room—how he found himself crying openly with these two girls who didn't understand and didn't want to have to understand that their mother might not see them graduate, marry, and have children. They might be pleased to give permission to tell their story if it would help others learn something from their personal struggle. Maybe they could learn something themselves.

Or perhaps he'd tell Jens Nilsson's story. Jens lost his job in a corporate shakeup and landed on the doorstep of the church late one night after a futile attempt to drink away his fear. Thirty years of board-room politics hadn't prepared him for the day he'd wake up without a job or a purpose.

Kathy Carswell had a story. She probably wouldn't want Jack to share the details, but he knew that as soon as he started talking, she'd start crying. Be it direct judgment or the indirect fallout of a world under curse, the church was full of people struggling to walk the fault lines.

Jack didn't think he'd have trouble connecting listeners with the message of this text. They could feel their world shaking.

—————

"Honey, I'll be a little late."

Fran Newman had heard this one before. She chose to be good-natured about it. It was part of the job, and it wouldn't help either of them for her to be cranky. "It's all right," she said. "The kids are all out playing. I didn't have anything special planned for dinner tonight."

Jack felt incredibly drawn to his wife at that moment. He didn't deserve her.

"Did you feel the earthquake?" she asked.

"What?" The question startled Jack. "How did you hear? Do you know about . . . ?"

"I caught Tom's report on the TV," she said.

Relieved, Jack recalled the tremors he had felt earlier, before the other news had shaken his life. "Knowing my brother, he turned it into something catastrophic."

"There wasn't any damage here, at least. Everything is safe and sound," Fran said.

Safe and sound. Warmer words could not have been spoken as Jack entered the hotel. Pastoral visitation had never been his favorite part of the job, but it had never seemed as uncomfortable as this.

Room 232, he was told. The hotel wasn't fancy. In fact, the place was downright seedy, as if to provide a kind of penance. He found the room and knocked. Some time passed before the door opened to reveal his friend, looking as haggard as one would expect. Jack extended his hand, almost automatically, then drew it back. Instead he moved toward his friend and embraced him. Chris Ellis was shaking, his arms limp, his spirit broken.

2

Footings

MAKE THE POINT

"I didn't know whether to hug him or hit him."

"I'd have hit him." Fran Newman was not sympathetic.

"No, you wouldn't have," Jack said. "He looked too pathetic."

"He is pathetic."

"He's still my friend."

"So you hugged him," Fran said dryly.

"I did," Jack admitted.

Fran softened. "That's what friends do." She admired her husband for his sensitivity. It's what made him a good pastor and a great husband.

"He didn't seem to appreciate it," Jack said. "It was awkward. He just stood limp for a moment, then pulled away. I don't think he really wanted to talk to me."

"But you tried anyway."

"Like you said, it's what friends do."

"Sometimes friends just listen," Fran added.

"I would have listened if there was something to listen to," Jack said. "He wouldn't say anything."

"Nothing?"

"He wouldn't even look at me. He just sat in the corner staring at the carpet," Jack said. "I tried to listen, you know—to give him room to find his voice—to let silence have its eloquence, but after a while, silence is just silent."

"How long did you stay?"

"Half an hour."

"And in all that time, he didn't say anything?"

"Not word one."

"So how did you leave it?"

"It was quiet. I don't think either of us could deal with it any more. I was all teary. He finally stood, and I did too. Even standing he looked sunken. I told him I'd be back. Then I left."

Fran moved toward her husband and touched his face, and he loved her for it.

The picture was crooked. Anna hadn't noticed it before. She had drawn the pencil-sketched sunset on her honeymoon with Henry. What was it, forty-seven years ago now? She couldn't remember at the moment.

"The picture is crooked," she said.

"I always liked that picture," Henry said from his spot on the sofa.

"It must have been the earthquake that skewed it," Anna said.

"I always thought the lack of color made it more intense, somehow."

"Like our marriage?" Anna meant it as a joke. It was the kind of thing that usually brought a chuckle from her good-natured husband.

Henry wasn't laughing.

Chloe Ellis tried the light switch, again. It was a small act of faith, offered in hope that the power company had done its job. Of course faith is only as good as its object. Still, you had to start somewhere, and despite their lousy track record, maybe the company had done its job and light would be restored.

Or not. Chloe would have to live in the dark a little longer. Not that she cared greatly. The dark hotel room suited her mood. The hotel staff was greatly embarrassed. Four-star hotels aren't supposed to offer their clients this kind of discomfort. Reports said the earthquake was small and inconsequential, but apparently it had caused some problems with the power grid near the airport.

Chloe's reaction to her husband's news had been to run. Feeling spiteful, she'd checked into the most expensive hotel she could find, even though she knew they couldn't afford it. Ironically, she'd heard that Chris was in a hotel as well—not this one of course. She'd checked. Not knowing where Chloe had gone, Chris apparently had decided that he'd better get out of the house before she got back. He wouldn't have wanted to face her anger—at least not right away. So now they were secluded in separate hotels. Chloe knew it was ridiculous, especially with the power problem, but she didn't want to go back. She was comfortable here—sort of—at least as comfortable as she could afford to be, given the circumstances. No one knew where she was. She wouldn't have to talk to anyone. Maybe later . . .

The phone startled her. It had a penetrating double ring, different from any of her phones at home. She picked up without thinking, regretting it instantly.

"Chloe?" Fran Newman said.

How did she find me?

"Chloe, are you there?"

Fran heard the line go dead.

The lights flickered on. Surprised, Chloe looked up to see her face in the giant hotel mirror. Long wet streaks cut darkly down her cheeks, her hair disheveled, her clothes wrinkled. She reached up and switched the lights again to darkness—darkness, to match her heart.

—⁓⁂⁓—

Tom Newman was squinting at his computer screen, a white Styrofoam cup of lukewarm coffee in his left hand, a pencil in his right hand, scribbling notes:

Earthquake:
- naturally induced shaking of the ground,
- caused by the fracture and sliding of rock within the Earth's crust.

6,000 earthquakes a year—global figures[1]
- 5,500 either too small or too far from populated areas to be felt.
- 450 are felt but cause no damage.
- 35 cause only minor damage.
- 15 a year cause death and suffering, damaging houses, buildings. . . .

Tom Newman didn't enjoy research. Yet his aversion to background work wasn't equal to his desire to appear well informed to his viewing public. God bless the Internet, he breathed to himself.[2]

On August 17, 1999, more than half a million people were left homeless in an earthquake in Istanbul. The problem was not so much the quake itself, as it was the quality of building construction in the city. Istanbul Governor Erol Cakir was quoted by CNN as saying that shoddy work by unscrupulous contractors may have contributed to the massive death toll in the magnitude 7.4 earthquake, which left tens of thousands in the ruins of collapsed buildings and caused the death of tens of thousands more.

On April 18, 1906, an earthquake lasting 48 seconds left the city of San Francisco in ruins. Much of the damage was done by fire, which destroyed the downtown area, leaving hundreds homeless. Masses of people converged on Golden Gate Park and area beaches looking for shelter and for help. Damages were estimated at $150 to $200 million!

In October 1989, San Francisco suffered another significant earthquake as fans gathered for game 3 of the World Series between the Oakland A's and the San Francisco Giants. As the crowd at Candlestick Park waited for the introduction of the starting lineups, an earthquake measuring 7.1 hit the Bay Area, shaking the ballpark and cutting electricity. Initially the mood was light until news reports of death and destruction from around the city began to come to the attention of fans listening on their radios.

In December 1988, a violent earthquake hit Armenia, the former Soviet state, killing more than fifty thousand people, most of whom were buried in the rubble of buildings that were unable to withstand the shaking. The problem would be exacerbated by extensive political unrest in the years to follow.

On January 25, 1989, just a few weeks after the first Armenian earthquake, a quake hit a different Armenia, the South American city of Armenia, Colombia. One month later, over 60 percent of the city was still in disrepair. The central district of the city was 90 percent destroyed. More than nine hundred people died, and those who were left lined the streets, living in makeshift tents and temporary shelters.

Tom hit the print button. He was particularly moved by the images—tattered children searching for family in the wreckage of buildings that wouldn't have been much to look at when in good repair, people with pickaxes working mounds of rubble searching for signs of life. It shamed him to think of his report from the airport the previous evening. The feeling was unfamiliar and uncomfortable. Maybe I should talk to somebody, he said to himself.

—⁂—

Make the Point . . .

Jack Newman was comfortable in his undersized and overstuffed office. The room was filled with cast-off furnishings recycled by well-meaning parishioners. Why was it that when people felt the need for something new at home they'd assume their rejected couch could continue to find service in the church youth wing or in the pastor's study. Jack entertained Old Testament images of unholy fire and rejected offerings, but only for a moment. Truth was, he didn't mind the lived-in look of his office fixtures. Besides, he didn't have the heart to criticize the people he loved so much.

He thought he'd use the half-hour before his next appointment to catch up on correspondence. Yet, somehow he couldn't rid himself of thoughts about his sermon. It had been like that a lot lately. Jack was learning to live his sermons. They consumed him, affecting his action and pestering his thoughts. No longer did he search the Scriptures looking only for something he could use to fill the slot on Sunday morning. Now he searched them in order that he might hear from God.

But it wasn't just the messages themselves. The very process and patterns of his preaching were changing the way he lived his life. He was learning to love the challenge of communication. He was growing to appreciate the intricacies of motivating people, not only to believe, but also to behave in accord with the great truths of Scripture.

For years in his ministry, he'd approach the weekend with no sermon prepared and no stamina to begin preparing. More than once he'd found himself scanning the Internet late Friday or even Saturday night, looking for a sermon to preach. He'd appease himself with the thought that, if the message was truth, it didn't really matter who had prepared it. People all over the web would gladly sell weeks of ready-made sermon outlines to a beleaguered preacher. They'd even throw in the illustrations for free.

It had been tempting. The people would never have to know—unless he chose to tell them. He could always do that. Jack had even heard of preachers who put citations in their bulletins to denote the sources of their sermons. He'd never been willing to go that far. Deep down he knew there'd be trouble if he let people know he was giving them other preachers' stuff. He remembered the blurb in *Christianity Today* reporting that pastors had lost their jobs after they'd been caught preaching plagiarized sermons. Parishioners surf the Internet too.[3]

It was an integrity issue, Jack admitted. It was also an issue of faithfulness to the call. He had never felt very good about the outcome whenever he'd preached someone else's sermon. There was something powerful about offering people the fruit of one's own study of the Word. To be able to listen for the voice of God, and then help others listen to the same message, was thrilling to Jack—now. He'd never take the easy route again.

Today's Sermon: Thou Shalt Not Steal

From Massachusetts to Texas, preachers have been caught delivering sermons verbatim—and without attribution—that they purchased from online and print sermons.

—St. Louis Post-Dispatch

The phone rang and Jack answered. "Yes, I'll have the announcements and the outline ready for the worship folder's order of worship by Thursday. . . . Yes, I heard you'll be taking care of the program while Janet's away on vacation. . . . Yes . . . Yes . . ." He was gracious. He kept his impatience hidden. A few minutes later he was able to hang up the phone and dig into his work.

Jack thumbed through his notes. He knew he'd be able to help the people sense the story behind his text. That wouldn't be a problem. His storytelling gifts would be sharpened by the events of recent days. He was confident that he could tap into the latent insecurity his listeners had squirreled away in hidden holes within their hearts.

But that wouldn't be enough. More than engaging the people in the story of the text, Jack needed to proclaim something. He'd have to teach them, to inform them. Jack would have to "make the point."

He'd been doing some reading on narrative preaching, but something about it left him dissatisfied. Affected by postmodern sensibilities, the writers tended to trust listeners to supply their own endings. Their sermons were like cartoon pictures published in a magazine without a caption. The reader must fill in the punch line. Preachers who deliberately leave their applications open-ended and undefined invite listeners to supply their own applications.

This philosophy sees it as the preacher's task to create experiential environments around God's Word that allow the listener to determine his or her own conclusion. This is consistent with a culture that rejects final answers and stern conclusions, but it's not helpful when one's task is to listen for God's voice in the text and proclaim his truth in the sermon.

A story's great, Jack reminded himself. It provides context and relevance for the listener, but it's still unfinished without a point. Proclamation is prejudiced—and that is a *good* thing. It's right that the preacher has a point and would want to present that point purposefully and even aggressively.

Jack thought again about Chris. What he'd done was wrong. People had been hurt, and it didn't have to be that way. Of course this situation was just one more instance of a scenario that was epidemic. Preachers needed to speak up and let the Word of God be heard. Some might think it arrogance and some might think it old fashioned, but Jack knew his people needed him to sound a sure and true word from the pulpit on Sunday. He needed it for his own heart.

So how does one make a point? Jack posed the question as a mental discipline, although he knew the answer well. Point making sorts out the mental categories so they make enough sense to produce a new way of thinking. Persuading a person to reorder their cognitive categories requires pertinent facts. Those facts need to be logically argued and clearly presented.

Make the Point

Explaining "What's What"

▶ Discern all the facts that are pertinent to the case that must be proved or the proposition that must be put.

▶ Lay out the argument so that it's reasonable and logical.

▶ Present the case as clearly as possible.

You start with the facts, not all the facts, but those relevant to the issue at hand. Sometimes, Jack knew, this is the real challenge of the sermon—to get the right data and to discern what is the important stuff. When it comes to preaching, of course, that means doing the exegetical homework. It might even mean spending time in the original language, diagramming sentence construction to settle on which are the major points and which are the minor points.

It means understanding the text theologically to insure that it is being read properly and given its rightful place in salvation history. It means listening carefully to the relevant arguments of experienced scholars and theologians, taking care not to distort their points or to mishear what they offer to the discussion. It means having the wisdom to know which ideas aren't worth considering and which will only confuse matters.

It means a lot of work, once you come to it. Jack's sigh was heavy.

The facts have to be made clear to the listener, which isn't always so easy. Jack knew the frustration of describing something that seemed clear to him, only to find that it had been as clear as a glass of Mississippi River water to some of his hearers. He always knew when he had blown it from the dazed look on Fran's face as they drove home after church.

Clarity requires using the listener's language and using it precisely. Clarity requires a judicious use of repetition. It requires the preacher to keep it simple and to say it slowly. It may require examples, metaphors, or illustrations that can unlock the idea without distracting the listener. Without clarity, the best arguments are indecipherable to the listener.

Of course, a boatload of facts won't convince anyone, even if they are clear. Persuasion requires the careful ordering of those facts so they're logically and reasonably presented. There's a place for faith and mystery in the Christian's understanding, but not at the expense of reason. Christians rely on both faith *and* reason to comprehend life, Jack reminded himself.

People may allow themselves to be swayed by irrationality, but logic always serves persuasion. A listener can reject reason, but only at reason's expense. Sometimes the gospel seems to transcend logic, or go beyond reason's limits. It was not *un*reasonable to believe in the incarnation of Christ. That Jesus existed with both divine and human natures is a mystery, in that it adheres to another level of logic, known only to the mind of God. A neat trick, some might say, but then that's what faith's for. Still, the preacher's responsibility is to present things sensibly and to offer the most convincing construction of the facts.

In the end, Jack knew, he had to cut through the clutter and get to the point—one point—one big idea the preacher could lock into the listener's mind. Occasionally, he'd offer three or four points in his sermon, but only if they were all in the service of the one big point. He'd learned through hard experience the critical importance of making that point clear. Jack had developed the habit of articulating his point in one "big idea theme statement." He liked to keep it down to ten words or less—with simple sentence construction so as to keep things focused. He was looking for a good aphorism that hadn't yet declined into cliché—all the better to hear with.

One Big Idea

- ▶ complete declarative sentence
- ▶ ten words or less
- ▶ one thought—no conjunctions

Having developed the point, Jack knew he had to communicate it, obviously and overtly. "Here's the thing we need to hear," he would say while preaching. "This is the one big thing we ought not miss from this passage in God's Word." In an oral presentation to a congregation populated with undisciplined daydreamers (and the odd avid listener), one had to be obvious and deliberate.

He shifted in his chair and checked his watch—still lots of time. Relieved, he returned to his thoughts.

Sometimes Jack felt the temptation to be "deep." He wasn't sure whether people were asking him to be "deep," but he occasionally thought he might like it if people were to conceive of him as profound in his preaching. The key, he knew, was not to confuse depth with complexity. Sermons ought to be challenging, but not difficult. They challenge in the sense that the sermon offers big thoughts that demand a response from the obedient listener. But if the sermon is difficult to listen to and overly complicated with points, understanding is not served. "Keep it simple," Jack repeated to himself.

All this isn't to say that people will be convinced, Jack knew. People are increasingly open to ambiguity. The most compelling case may have little power for someone who just doesn't feel like changing.

That's what makes it interesting, Jack thought to himself. Still, a person has to decide to reject a point if it's forcefully made.

"If I make my point," he whispered, "the truth has to be reckoned with."

His cell phone cut into his reverie, surprising him. He usually turned it off to conserve the battery when he came into the office.

"Jack, this is Terri Jones, your brother Tom's personal assistant."

"Oh, yes, I remember you," Jack answered warmly. One didn't forget someone as attractive as Terri Jones.

"Tom was wondering if you were available later this afternoon. He says he wants to talk to you."

"Looking for a little brotherly advice, no doubt."

"He's been a little grumpy as far as I'm concerned," Terri complained. "Maybe you could help us out with that."

"I'll see what I can do," Jack said with a chuckle.

———

Chloe didn't bother with her makeup before leaving the room. It struck her as she stepped onto the sidewalk that it had been years since she'd been outdoors without at least some blush. Maybe on that camping trip at Yellowstone last year? No, Chris had given her a hard time because she'd brought her cosmetics bag into the tent. She remembered him saying that the lip gloss would attract the bears, like he knew what would attract bears. Chloe smiled, despite herself. Fishing around in her bag, she found a pair of dark glasses. The day wasn't bright, but she'd wear her sunglasses anyway.

She entered the bookstore uncertainly—so many people. What if someone recognized her? She'd made sure to go across town where she'd be less likely to see or be seen by anyone, but still. . . . She remembered running into a neighbor on Waikiki Beach when she was with Chris in Hawaii on their tenth anniversary vacation.

She scanned the store. If people don't read anymore because of television and movies you sure couldn't tell it by this place. Then again, the books she scanned all seemed to be movie related. There were books written from movies, or books that were made into movies, or books about movies, or books about movie stars, or books by movie stars . . . but that was only the first four rows. The place was huge.

"Chloe?" Fran Newman hadn't expected to run into the woman who'd been dominating her thoughts lately.

"Fran," Chloe stammered, unable to conceal her disappointment—and her fear.

"I didn't expect to see you here."

"I'm sorry, Fran, I wasn't expecting to see anyone either."

"You were hoping you wouldn't see anyone. . . ."

"Oh, no-o, I just meant . . ."

"It's okay, I understand," Fran reassured her friend. "I know what you must be going through . . . well . . . actually I don't know what you're going through, . . . but I've been thinking a lot about you lately, and it just seems amazing that we'd bump into each other at the bookstore of all places; probably one of those 'God things' . . . but, no, I'm sorry, I'm making too much of a chance encounter, when you just want to be alone. . . ."

Fran hadn't meant to run off at the mouth, but sometimes when you start a sentence it's difficult to know how to end it.

"I just came to get something to read, you know, something distracting." Chloe Ellis turned and started moving toward the door. "But thank you, Fran," she said, "it's just . . . awkward. Maybe in a few days or a few weeks . . ." Her smile was feeble.

Fran Newman watched her leave, "Wait, Chloe," she exclaimed. "You didn't get a book."

Chloe stopped and paused before turning. Her eyebrows were twisted in half-exasperation. Her face softened. "Maybe you could suggest something," she said, offering a tentative invitation.

Fran stepped forward with confidence and took her friend by the arm. "My husband says I'm always full of suggestions. Here, let's have a cup of coffee."

The upscale coffee shop was a prominent section of the bookstore. Tables were crowded, and the two women had to stand against the wall with their coffee in their hands while they waited for a spot. Two preteen girls were giggling over fashion magazines at one table. The fact that they hadn't bought anything and clearly didn't intend to buy anything did nothing to weaken their presumption. It was annoying.

"I called yesterday," Fran offered, "at the hotel."

"Was that you?" Chloe asked. "How did you know I was there?"

"I guessed. I remembered the banquet we all attended there last year, and you mentioned how much you liked the hotel. You said you'd love to stay there if you ever got the chance. It seemed funny at the time. People don't normally stay in hotels in their own city."

"Not normally," Chloe said. "But I guess this isn't a normal circumstance, is it?"

"I suppose not," Fran replied, "but you might be surprised."

"Apparently I'm easily surprised. . . . I always thought I'd notice if anything like this were ever to happen in our marriage. Not that I thought about it much. I just thought that somehow two people in an intimate relationship would send signals. I'm angry with myself for not recognizing it. I hate that I was surprised. I hate that I was that obtuse."

"None of us saw it coming."

A table opened up, and Chloe and Fran were quick to take advantage. Fran perched on a stool up against the window. Chloe sunk, lower than expected, into an overstuffed chair. The eclectic furniture, intended for ambiance, was all that was available.

"It's not uncommon to hear about pastors messing around." Fran was trying to be encouraging.

"That's not comforting," Chloe said.

"No," Fran agreed.

"What's wrong with these guys?" Chloe sounded exasperated. "I mean, I understand that other women look at them as high and holy. I understand that something about the position itself might attract some women. They see our husbands as paragons of spirituality, and there's something subliminally sexy about that. They come off as understanding, comforting, and caring."

"I understand it from the woman's point of view," Fran agreed. "But I'm angry at the men, these husbands who can't keep their pants zipped. They ought to know better. They ought to be able to anticipate . . . to take precautions." Fran surprised herself with her intensity.

The Message Comes from God

Preachers don't come from some exalted place of knowledge. They come from the pew. But the message they preach doesn't come from the pew. It comes from God.[4]

—**Charles Bartow,** *God's Human Speech,* 19

Chloe was opening up now. "I always loved Chris, not only for his strength, but also for his weakness. Chris really loved God, and I loved him for it. Yet, at the same time, I was there with him late at night in bed when he'd voice his doubts. Sometimes I'd find him up at 1 or 2 Sunday morning before he had to preach. It was agony for him at times trying to connect with God so he could say something helpful to the people the next morning."

"I know about that," Fran said.

"Then, I'd see him get up into the pulpit just a few hours later and preach so powerfully. I've seen God move in dramatic ways at times, even in my own heart, when I've watched my husband in such spiritual agony over the delivery. It's almost like he's in labor, having sermon contractions. . . ."

Finally there was laughter.

"It's just so hard to understand how God could speak through a human so flawed."

"And yet you loved, I mean, you *love* him," Fran said.

"I loved him," Chloe corrected.

"And God loves him," Fran said.

Both of them were silent for a moment as that thought sank in.

"There is something mysterious about it," Fran agreed. "I didn't want Jack to be a pastor. I didn't need the pressure.

"*We* didn't need the pressure, and I'm not just talking about the pressure other people put on us, but the pressure we put on ourselves.

I expect a lot of Jack. I want him to live up to his calling. I want him to be the spiritual giant people expect preachers to be."

"He's not," Chloe said. "He might not be Chris, but he's not God either."

Fran wasn't sure she wanted to respond to that one.

"I find it incredibly mysterious," Chloe added.

"What?"

"That God would use people like Chris and people like Jack . . ."

". . . and people like you and me . . . "

". . . to speak his Holy Word."

Was it Fran's imagination, or had the coffee shop atmosphere quieted for just a moment. "It's pretty cool, isn't it?"

"It really is," Chloe admitted. "It would seem more cool if Chris just weren't so massively stupid!"

Jack reported to the station's news department, where Terri Jones greeted him warmly. She had one of those hands-free telephone headsets embedded in her flowing, wavy hair. "Go on in, he's waiting for you."

"I don't imagine we'll be too long," Jack replied.

"Take him as long as you want . . . please!" Terri mocked.

The newsroom was noisy. Jack had trouble imagining how Tom could accomplish any work in such an environment. The church offices were loud and busy from time to time, but at least he could close his office door so he could concentrate. Then again, Tom wasn't trying to write sermons here.

"Jack," Tom called. With his ear still attached to a telephone he reached around the divider to pull a chair from the next cubicle and motioned for Jack to sit. Jack waiting patiently for Tom to finish what appeared to be a one-sided conversation. Eventually, he grunted and hung up the phone.

"Nice phone manners," Jack teased. "Didn't mom teach you any better than that?"

"What, that? It was nothing—management, you know."

"So when are they going to give you a real office. I'd have thought an anchorman would rate something more substantial than this."

"What would I do with an office? I'm seldom here. The mobile broadcast van is my real office."

"Or is it that cardboard set you sit behind every evening?"

"I think it's management's way to keep me active. They don't want me too comfortable. News happens on the street, not behind a desk."

"And I thought you were just another pretty face."

"Somebody in our family ought to be pretty." Tom decided not to laugh. "Can we go somewhere, buddy, somewhere we can talk?"

They left the building and crossed the street. There was an unoccupied bench in the adjacent courtyard. Tom examined it before sitting down. "What are you worried about?" Jack teased. "Nobody sees your pants on camera."

Maybe it was the timing. Neither brother's humor was hitting the mark. Tom's face tightened. "What do you think of what I do?" Tom asked.

Jack looked carefully into his brother's eyes before answering. Clearly he was serious. "You mean your job?"

"My job, life, *vocation*...."

"Vocation." Jack paused thoughtfully. "That's a heavy word. It comes from the Latin *vox* or 'voice.' It suggests the idea of *calling*. If it is a calling, it means someone has a plan. It suggests that we do what we do in service to God."

"I've always thought of news reporting in those terms," Tom said, "not that I was trying to be religious about it. It just seemed that my job mattered—that I was fulfilling an important duty, in service of the public, in service of..."

"... the truth?"

Tom looked away. "I guess that's what's bothering me. I've always tried to do solid news. I wanted to be trustworthy. When I looked into the camera I wanted people to believe in me and in what I was saying. The network even advertises that way, putting my face on billboards, marketing my integrity to pull market share and advertisers."

"If you can't trust your news anchor, who can you trust?"

"Maybe your preacher," Tom said.

"Are you serious?" Jack asked, not sure if this was another example of his brother's questionable wit.

"Nothing is what it seems to be," Tom said. "It's all in presentation. We choose what we show the public and how we show it. Stability, instability, hope, hatred—it's all a matter of perspective. The world's such a big, complex place, and it just seems pathetic that people like me are looked to for footings. We can't make much sense of it either. They should be looking to you."

Jack wasn't sure what to say.

"What are you preaching on this Sunday?"

"Excuse me?"

"Come on," Tom said. "Don't look so shocked. What are you preaching? Tell me something certain. Tell me something I can trust."

"Hebrews 12," Jack answered. "It's actually quite timely, given the ruckus you created about that tremor at the airport."

Tom looked interested. "The text uses the image of an earthquake to describe the instability of not just the earth, but the people, the institutions, even the ideas that are in it. I suppose it's addressing just the thing you've been talking about. It's all fragile, everything we count on for life, security, and stability. One good shake can bring the whole thing crashing down."

"That's what people are afraid of," Tom agreed. "Stability is critical to our economic security. Our society thrives when we feel like things are under control. When it starts to feel shaky, markets dive, and everybody runs for cover. We're running a report out of Wall Street tonight, how it reacts with such volatility to the day's headlines."

"The text goes further. It's describing a more ominous kind of shaking," Jack slowed his rate of speech. He wasn't sure how his brother would take what he wanted to say. He chose his words cautiously. "It talks about judgment."

"What? Armageddon?" Tom tried to look skeptical. It was an automatic reaction, which didn't feel authentic this time.

"Well, something like that. The Bible says that one day God is going to stand up and speak. When he does, everything on earth will feel his wrath, like a great shaking. . . ."

"You mean literally?"

"Maybe. I can't tell you exactly what it'll be like, but the Bible says that when God shakes the earth, everything unstable and impure will break off and fall away. Everything the world looks to for security will be shown for what it is."

"Sounds like bad news."

"Not entirely. The Bible never offers bad news without supplying better news as well. The good news is that God has provided for our security. There is a safe place to stand—one sure thing that won't be affected—a refuge in the eye of the storm. The Bible says God's kingdom is the one thing that cannot be shaken and, as long as we are attached to that, nothing can touch us. We're secure. We're strong. We're. . . ."

Jack was surprising himself with the depth of his own conviction. He felt his sails filling, his confidence building. He thought about the pain of the last several days. He thought about Chris and Chloe. He thought about what his brother had been asking—his successful, messed-up brother. Jack felt full of uninhibited confidence. He felt he wanted to stand up like some old-fashioned street evangelist. He felt like preaching.

The ground moved—*literally*.

Later, Jack would reflect on the timing. It was as if it had been scripted—as if God had punctuated the critical moment in their conversation. At the moment, though, all Jack and Tom did was react automatically. Jack grabbed his brother's arm and pulled him back down to sit.

Tom looked uncertain. He gripped the bench firmly. The uncertainty wasn't long-lived. The concrete below their feet split with a loud crack. The bench, no longer fixed securely, lurched backward, spilling the brothers to the ground. Windows were breaking in nearby buildings, sounding like small explosions. Glass was flying. One large shard struck Jack in the leg, opening a gash. None of the buildings fell, at least not in their entirety. Dust was blowing up and the sky had grown remarkably dark. The brothers ran, though they were unsure where to run. Tom's cell phone was ringing. The newsman didn't notice.

Fran Newman was looking at magazines when the earthquake struck. She felt so good about her conversation with Chloe—not that she'd made a pivotal difference, solving all of Chloe's problems. It just felt like Fran had helped, that she had been a friend, and that it had been appreciated. Trying to prolong the moment, she'd taken her leisure in the bookstore. She could use something new to read, perhaps something fun.

A magazine fell beside her feet. She bent to pick it up when another fell to her left, opening to reveal a promiscuous looking woman in a full-page spread. A third magazine fell, and then several more. Fran looked up just in time to see the bookshelf come down. She shot herself forward with an athleticism she hadn't known for many years. It wasn't enough.

Chloe Ellis was trying to unlock her car, but she couldn't seem to insert her key into the lock. She didn't think she was that upset. In fact, after her conversation with Fran, she felt calmer than she'd been in days, except that her hand was shaking, or maybe—could it be the car?

Screams from the bookstore helped her realize what was happening. Then all she could think about was Fran. Impulsively she ran back inside. Shelves had fallen and people seemed frantic. Startled staff attempted to impose some sort of order. Chloe ignored them. She was looking for her friend.

Fran's head was the only visible part of her body, which was lying twisted. Chloe found her pinned under a fallen bookshelf, with magazines strewn around. Blood oozed onto a crinkled motorcycle magazine beneath her head. Chloe felt sick as she checked to see if Fran was breathing. She was.

The shelves were heavy. The expensive dark wood shelving gave the bookstore a high-end ambiance. Chloe cursed their obstinate weight as she tried to move them. The store was emptying quickly, and no one seemed to notice what she was doing. Chloe grabbed at a thickset man as he ran past, but he slipped her grasp. Her cries got the attention of a young woman wearing the bookstore's logo badge that announced her name to be Kristen. "Can I help you?" The words came out as a trained response, but they didn't match the look of fear upon her face.

Chloe seized the salesperson and pulled her around so that she could see Fran Newman lying unconscious on the floor. Kristen snapped from her daze and started barking orders. Sirens were sounding in the distance as the two women strained to move the bookshelf. Using all their strength they could lift it, but neither could support its weight while the other pulled Fran to safety. Chloe was starting to cry, and Kristin wasn't far behind when they felt the weight suddenly become lighter. A strong young man was lifting the other corner. Chloe let go of her end and pulled Fran from beneath the bookshelf.

———◄▒▒◊▒▒►———

Henry Ellis was on his way to set up chairs at the church. Someone else would do it if he didn't show up. They might have to start their meeting five minutes late, but they could set out their own chairs if they had to. Henry didn't really feel much like working at the church, but it was what he did. It was his responsibility. He'd agreed to it, and life had to go on.

No sense moping around the house. He ought to do what he always did. The sooner he could get back into his routines, the sooner he'd feel better, or so he told himself.

He was having trouble holding the road, and instantly recognized the feel of an earthquake. He turned the corner just in time to see the steeple fall. Funny what you think of at times like this. As he watched the support crumble and the tower slowly ease from its foundation, he remembered the job of replacing that roof. To save money, they had recruited a volunteer work party. They did a great job on the flat parts, but their inexperience had shown at the edges and corners. The steeple was a bear. They could not get the flashings right and eventually called in a professional roofer to fix their work. They probably hadn't saved much in the end.

The steeple didn't so much fall as tumble. It turned lengthwise, end over end, hitting the ground upside down, so that the pointed top imbedded itself into the earth like a giant tent peg. The rest of the structure crumbled. The old brick and mortar wasn't up to the stress of shifting supports.

It was like a bomb had gone off. Henry thought of film clips of a building being deliberately demolished by controlled detonations to force the walls to fall inward. A cloud of dust rose as the building imploded. This was like that, Henry decided, just like that.

Henry got out of his car and looked in wonder at the pile of rubble in front of him. It had all happened so fast. Six decades of ministry. Countless pitch-in meals. There it was, three stories that had absorbed six decades and thousands of sermons, reduced to a heap.

Henry had cried when he first heard the news about Chris, and now he cried again.

3

Frailty

ENGAGE THE PROBLEM

"Excuse me, sir. You can't go in there."

Jack Newman wasn't wearing his hospital ID.

"It's okay. I'm Pastor Newman. I'm part of the chaplaincy team. You can check the list. I didn't think to pick up my ID."

The woman was new. "I'm sorry, pastor. Everyone is supposed to have a badge in this part of the hospital."

"But it's my wife. They called to tell me she's here. Her name is Fran."

"Just a minute, sir," the woman turned to answer the phone.

This was different, Jack realized. He'd been here so many times, but never in this role. He was the guy on the other side of the conversation, who held the hand of the harried husband. Now he was that husband, and a frightened one.

"Pastor?"

Jack was relieved to see a familiar face. Molly Shires came with her husband to the church when she wasn't on a Sunday morning nursing shift. "Molly, can you help me out here?" he asked.

"It's okay," she said to the desk attendant, "I can vouch for him." The nurse took Jack through the door and down a wide corridor. There were people everywhere, in wheelchairs, on gurneys, or leaning against a wall. Some were obviously injured. Others appeared to be sleeping. Some moaned in obvious discomfort as they waited for medical attention. Fran Newman's name wasn't on her list, but Molly had recognized her when the ambulance brought her in. Now where did they put her?

A few people looked hopefully as they passed and one grabbed at Jack's arm begging for help, evidently assuming that he was an off-duty doctor just arriving. Molly was opening doors, searching blindly, until they found Fran in an out-of-the-way hallway along one of the more dingy looking walls of the old section. She seemed to be sleeping, Jack thought, until he came around the other side of the bed and saw the large bandage on the back of her skull. The dark stain indicated that her scalp had been bleeding.

"All this happened in a bookstore?"

"You'd be surprised what happens to people in an earthquake," Molly said. "They're stacked up like firewood in the ER."

"Is it bad?" Jack asked.

"You mean your wife?" The nurse checked her list once more to see if any information had magically appeared. "I have to get back on duty, but let me see if I can find someone who knows something," Molly said. She was wearing her "professional care" face. Jack wondered if she was pushing to the side her own worries about husband or family.

He didn't know how he should feel, sitting alone in the hallway, waiting. Nearby noises reverberated uncomfortably, and the stifling heat seemed devoid of oxygen. Instinct told him to find someone to yell at. He wanted action. His wife needed help. But what do you do when demand outstrips supply?

His attention turned to his wife as she stirred. He should pray. That's what he'd do if he had come as pastor and not victim. Yes, he should pray. But as he bowed his head no words came. He was left without a prayer.

Tom Newman was all business, and business was brisk. His mobile broadcast center was equipped as a field command post to handle breaking news like this, and it was in full operation now. A portable fax machine, plugged into the small generator, was spitting out reports and technical data from the City Central Meteorological Office. His laptop, mounted in a bracket designed for the purpose, was attached to a cell phone, creating a wireless Internet connection—too slow for his liking, but good enough. A GPS satellite positioning monitor mounted to the dashboard showed points of critical damage. Tom's hands-free headset fed voice commands to a second cell phone. Cell phone networks usually failed in a disaster. The system overloaded when everyone called everyone else at the same time. Already, radio announcers urged people to avoid using their phones except for serious emergencies. "I thought that's why people bought cell phones—for security in emergencies," Tom said to his partner in the back of the car.

Bob Wilson grunted. He was busy in the rear seat, attending to his equipment, installing fresh tapes in cameras, labeling and stowing spent cassettes. He was a professional—a good man to have in a crisis.

"We need a plan," Tom said. "I could run around all day like this. It's like Beirut out here."

Wilson smiled at Tom's hyperbole. The anchor portrayed calm and control on the air, but his friend was anything but calm when he wasn't "on camera."

"Divide up the major disaster points. Send Harker to cover everything north of the highway. Tell Shin to handle whatever's happening east of downtown. I'll . . ." He consulted the GPS readout, pushing the zoom button for a larger readout. "I'll cover the southwest section. I'm not far from . . ."

The broadcaster cut off his sentence as the vehicle swung around the corner. Tom had actually seen the devastation in Beirut, Lebanon, during the civil conflict there. This was different, of course, but the comparison wasn't entirely ridiculous. A highway on-ramp had dropped. The west wall of a warehouse had collapsed, as if someone had driven a bomb-laden vehicle into its side.

But the sight that stopped his sentence was set directly in front of him. Three new high-rise apartments had been built on the west edge of downtown. Marketed to the middle-upper-income demographic, the units were created to look like the trendy habitat of wealthy young urbanites. Acres of shiny steel and glass towered over an expanse of parkland. High-speed Internet cable was piped to every room. Flat-screen wall-mounted high definition television came standard in every unit.

The project had sold quickly. A banner had been hung just the previous week declaring the buildings to be more than 75 percent sold. What Tom saw now took his breath away. Every window was shattered. Building 3 had sunk to its knees, a full five stories shorter than it had been a few hours earlier. The "sold" banner was torn and flopping raggedly in the wind like a revolutionary flag. Bits of furniture and other unidentified rubble were strewn along the roadside.

"I think we've got something," Tom said, as he pulled the vehicle up to the curb. The feeling was eerie. *I haven't seen anything like this since 9/11,* Tom thought. Of course nothing would be like that—or so he hoped.

Bob Wilson had jumped out before the car had even come to a stop, already sizing up the best angle. The sun would set in an hour, which would make for a dramatic shot.

Tom wasn't looking forward to meeting his assistant with this news: "Terri, about your new apartment . . ."

Chloe felt jammed into the crowded hospital waiting room. She couldn't get in with Fran. The hospital people were too busy to deal with civilians who weren't even related to the injured. She could go back to the hotel, but what would she do there? She really had nowhere to go, and even though it was intolerably cramped, she'd rather be near her friend in case she needed someone.

A ceiling-mounted television was tuned to Cable News Network (CNN). The *Breaking News* banner was displayed across the bottom of the screen. It's not often that one's home city becomes the focus of national attention, she said to herself. Of course, to be in the national media spotlight usually had catastrophic implications. *We'll be hearing nothing but earthquake stories for days,* she mused tiredly.

On TV, a graphic displayed statistics for the worst of a century of earthquakes.[1]

- Tangshan, China, 1976—255,000 dead
- Gansu, China, 1920—200,000 dead
- Nanshan, China, 1927—2,000,000 dead
- Yokohama, Japan, 1923—143,000 dead
- Messina, Italy, 1980—83,000 dead
- Gansu, China, 1932—70,000 dead
- Northern Peru, 1970—66,000 dead

Chloe amused herself with the mental note not to make plans to vacation in Gansu. Of course, other people's misery seldom made one feel much better about one's own, but it did give a little perspective, Chloe admitted.

I wonder if anyone has died here today? I wonder about Fran? She dismissed the thought.

Sighing, Chloe stood to stretch and noticed a man leaving the hospital through the doors on the other side of the room. It was too crowded to get close enough to tell, but it looked like Jack Newman. It would be great if he'd gotten word.

But why is he leaving? Is that good news or bad? She couldn't decide. Pushing through the crowd, she got to the door just as the man was pulling out of the parking lot. It did look like Jack. Maybe something had happened. She'd ask at the desk and try to get some information.

Chloe got into the lengthy line at the information desk with a curious mix of apathy and impatience. The line wasn't really moving. She felt a tear forming on her face. The sight of Jack had awakened an uncomfortable thought that she had been trying to avoid—*Chris.* She spoke his name under her breath. Had anything happened to Chris?

Jack Newman was back in his car, driving madly. He really should stay with Fran, he told himself again, yet he didn't think he could stand another minute in that hallway. Molly Shires had finally found a doctor willing to talk to Jack, but of course he didn't have much to say. It was a matter of waiting. She seemed to be stable—a serious concussion but without signs of internal bleeding. These things usually come out all right, he added, but it was too soon to say. They'd keep checking on her, and they were trying to discharge patients to open more rooms. Molly also was encouraging. She promised to keep a close eye on Fran, and she wasn't going off duty any time soon. So he should try to relax. Maybe get some sleep. She took down his cell number. "I'll call right away if anything happens."

Yes, sleep, Jack thought. *Sleep is good, except it isn't likely to happen.*

His thoughts turned to the church. How many needed their pastor? He should be available. People relied on him. He almost welcomed the familiar feelings of guilt, which distracted from the danger of his wife's condition.

He was halfway home before he realized that his phone had not been ringing. That was surprising, given what was going on. He checked the power, only to see that he had forgotten to turn the phone back on after leaving the hospital. Jack slammed his hand against the steering wheel. If he wasn't a pastor, he might have cursed himself. He called the church, but the line was dead. He couldn't even get through to the machine. That was funny. He called home and punched in the code to pick up his messages. Henry had called. He sounded worried. Jack called up Henry's number and pressed the keypad accordingly. He was having some trouble keeping the vehicle straight on the road while punching numbers.

"Jack," Henry's voice was louder than normal. "You've got to get to the church right away."

"What is it, Henry?"

"Just come, Jack. Come quickly."

Jack made a sharp U-turn, narrowly missing a car coming too quickly up the left-hand lane. The woman driver shot Jack an angry look. Jack's face reddened with recognition. The woman was Terri Jones.

Terri was frustrated. No, she was angry. The police had barricaded the road to her condominium several blocks back. She'd have to walk, once she found a parking spot. She should have brought station press credentials.

It might have been helpful if she had. Police sometimes gave media access through a blockade—if they had credentials.

She circled the block, vainly looking for a place to stop. Turning north on Sixty-fourth Street, she caught sight of what was left of her building. She'd been so proud of her new condominium. It had been a stretch to qualify for the mortgage, but Tom had a contact, a mortgage broker who knew how badly the developers needed to sell this new building. Terri stopped on the road, oblivious to the few drivers in the area that were honking their horns and pulling awkwardly around her. She didn't see their angry glances or hear their shouts. Her head was pressed forward, her face turned toward where her seventh-floor window should have been. Terri was tough, and her job had made her tougher. But she wasn't sure how she could handle this. Not now.

Her car lurched forward as she heard the sickening sound of collapsing metal. Her seatbelt probably saved her from more serious injury, but her face smacked the glass with a bruising thud. It occurred to her that a newer car would have had airbags. She was still dazed when she heard the policeman knock on her window.

Terri hadn't wanted to go to the hospital. She wanted to go to her apartment. She wanted to find Tom. The officer had talked her into being checked out. There was nothing she could do about the apartment. They weren't letting anyone—including residents—near the building. Right now, she needed to get medical attention. Rear-end accidents can do serious damage to a person's spine.

He really was very kind, she thought, as she started to climb into the backseat of the police car. She was surprised to see that the seats were molded plastic. There were no handles on the inside of the door, and the glass between the front and back seat looked thick enough to stop bullets. She was just sitting down when the officer changed his mind. "You don't have to sit back there," he said. He brought her around to the frontseat to ride the few blocks to the hospital.

The emergency room was overcrowded, as she had expected. She might have waited all night if the police officer hadn't gotten the attention of a senior nurse, who found Terri a bed behind a curtain, a minor miracle, and promised a prompt visit from a doctor.

How long she waited there she couldn't tell. It might have been minutes. It might have been hours. All she knew was that she hadn't cried like this in years.

⸺⦿⸻

"So what'll we do on Sunday?" Henry Ellis voiced the question that had been nagging at Jack.

"We could cancel services," Jack said tentatively, almost as a question aimed at Henry. The response was a frown.

"I don't know what else to do, Henry. The building's gone, and the city's a mess. How will we ever rent a facility large enough this late in the week?"

Grudging silence indicated that Henry didn't have an answer he liked any better. They'd spent some time poking around in the rubble, until the police who were stringing barrier tape strongly suggested that the fire department had better secure the site before someone was hurt. No matter; it appeared that there was little to salvage. The two friends drifted toward a nearby fast-food restaurant to talk. Even then, they sat in shocked silence for some time.

"We could call Grace Community, I imagine. They'd have plenty of room in their sanctuary. We could encourage everyone to join in with them. Maybe we could arrange a joint prayer service. Though, I'm not sure how many would go that far."

"What about Friendship Neighborhood Church?" Henry suggested. "The pastor's an old friend."

"That might be better. Maybe they could add a service. All I know is, I don't think I could preach this Sunday, even if we had somewhere to meet."

"Fran?" Henry asked.

"Fran . . . Chris . . . The building . . . Me. I'm just not in a place where I think I could preach," Jack said. "The whole idea feels abhorrent at the moment."

Henry didn't respond. He had to admit he didn't feel a lot different. He knew how glad he was he didn't have to preach this Sunday. That was one of the hardest things about serving as a pastor, he reflected. You never got a break. It didn't matter what happened in the world or in your private world—you still had to preach. You could be feeling great or you could be feeling lousy, but you had to get up in that pulpit, and the sermon had better be invigorating or they'd be roasting you for dinner. Henry looked at Jack and felt his pain. *Retirement has its privileges,* he told himself.

"It's ironic," Jack said.

"What's ironic, Jack?"

"My sermon this Sunday," he said. "I was so excited about it. It was so perfect for this Sunday. It still is, I guess, if someone else were to preach it. . . ." He pondered for a while. "You know how great it is when you hear from God in his Word. I love it when I can dig into the Scriptures and emerge with a clear sense of exactly what God wants me to say through *this* text to *these* people at *this* time."

"It's what a preacher lives for," Henry said.

"But sometimes it isn't enough."

"Meaning?"

"Sometimes the clearest truths just lie flat for me," Jack said. "I'm smart enough to recognize the truth, and I know enough to believe it, but sometimes it doesn't seem to go far enough."

"Keep talking."

"I see it in my people all the time, but now and then I see it in myself. It scares me. So often we sit in the sanctuary and listen to the sermon. We nod in all the right places and affirm all the right things. We do it because we understand that truth is true, and we appreciate the need to build our lives on something firm. Yet, at the same time, we struggle with truth's reality in our lives. I get the feeling sometimes that the clearer and neater the sermon, the less I understand its relevance to my own life situation."

"You want messy sermons, Jack? I've preached a few of those in my time."

"Not homiletically messy, Henry. I'm not talking about poorly constructed sermons. I mean sermons that are real enough to recognize the mysteries and to struggle with the realities. Preachers hate to admit that there's a problem with just about everything they say. They want to package truth in tidy three-point packages, but life isn't tidy, and everybody knows it. The more airtight our sermons feel, the less authentic they seem to people who live the mess life presents."

"Messy" Preaching

Relevance?

Tidy Sermons ◄————————————► Untidy Lives

"I think I'm tracking with you," Henry said. "I might put it theologically. We preach the Bible. The Bible as a word from God is a word to us. In some ways it's a word *against* us. We don't easily surrender to a message from God's Word. Some struggle usually is involved."

"A *whole lot* of struggling ought to be involved," Jack said, sweeping his hands apart a little too dramatically. His soft drink gushed across the table, spilling liquid across the floor and spreading ice cubes like gravel across a driveway.

Henry laughed, then tried to choke it off. But this laugh had been a long time coming. He let himself laugh hard, glad for some kind of emotional release. Jack, however, didn't join him.

"Why don't we walk?" Jack said, not waiting to hear an answer. Henry scrambled out of his seat, quickly trying to clean up the mess while Jack prepared to leave the restaurant. He probably would have left it as it was, but he stooped down anyway and tried to help Henry until a perky staff member came along with a mop and told them not to worry. The employee even handed Jack a fresh drink, which he wasn't sure he really wanted.

Outside, the sky was darkening. The air was cooling. *Winter's coming,* Jack thought as he zipped his jacket to the top. The two men walked for a few minutes without saying anything. Jack was taking the lead, though he wasn't sure where he was leading them.

"Sometimes I feel I ought to be more aggressive in my preaching," he said.

Henry wasn't sure what he meant.

"I think we're far too tame in the way we preach," Jack continued. "I don't mean we should attack our listeners or make the experience unpleasant."

"Maybe it should be unpleasant sometimes. An occasional unpleasant sermon might have more integrity."

"Well, sure, that's what I mean. Why do we think sermons ought to be easy? We're so predictable. How often do you leave the sanctuary feeling smug because you've already heard and have committed, at least intellectually, to everything the preacher is saying? If we really want to affect change—if we truly want to get through to people—we have to get under their skin. Real change happens deep inside people's hearts, and it isn't easy to get down inside there. People have it locked down and buried over with all kinds of garbage. I'm thinking that many of our sermons slip across the surface without really taking root in the listener's soul."

"Teflon listeners."

"Exactly. No-stick sermons offered fresh every Sunday."

"So you want to be more aggressive in your preaching," Henry said. "I can understand that. But how are you going to do it without offending your congregation? Aren't you afraid you'll turn them all away?"

"I suppose that depends on how it's done," Jack said. "Aggressive preaching won't be boring, that's for sure. I'm thinking that people turn away from preaching more because it doesn't engage them. A sermon that challenges them will at least capture their attention."

"I've heard a fair bit of yelling from pulpit-pounders who demand that I shape up or ship—"

"That's not what I'm talking about," Jack interrupted. "Most of those guys come off as irrelevant, especially to the contemporary listener. I'm not talking about attacking listeners. We have to love the listener, but we have to have some passion about what we're asking of them. I'm talking about forcing the encounter, aggressively speaking to stuff the listener has kept buried. I'm talking about being so relevant that listeners can't slip away, or don't want to slip away—getting them by the scruff of the neck, so to speak, where they're transfixed, because they realize they have to do business with the message God is offering."

"It sounds almost violent."

"You know what makes aggressive preaching work? I have to be preaching to myself. The message has to have me by the throat. If we're all caught together in the challenge, listening to God, then it can create an incredible moment. We are all ready together to see something amazing happen."

Henry pondered that for a moment. "There's an awful lot at stake," he said.

"Yes!" Jack punctuated his agreement. "Sometimes my knees get weak just thinking about what God might have in mind, how things could change. I'm like Isaiah, looking for the smoke and the fire, waiting to see the doorposts shake."

"Maybe you need to grow a beard," Henry said. "Go for that prophetic Old Testament look."

"I'm getting so tired of going through the motions when people's lives are falling apart out there, just like our building. When I think of Chris . . ." Jack had trouble finishing his sentence.

"I know," Henry said.

"I just don't know if I have the heart for it *this* Sunday."

"You expressed it with a lot of feeling just now."

Jack pondered his response. "I'm just not sure I can actually do it this time. I'm not sure I'm strong enough to be that honest with myself before God. Not if I want it to be *real*."

Henry understood. He understood too well.

―――

Jack woke with the shaking. Aftershock? Not again! No, a piece of heavy medical equipment was being wheeled down the hall by a pair of supersized hospital orderlies. Jack had left the immediate care of things in Henry's hands. The building was destroyed, of course. An appointment with the insurance people was scheduled for tomorrow. He was surprised that they were able to respond that quickly, but they needed to see the extent of the damage first hand. So far as he knew, Fran was the only person in the congregation injured or displaced in the earthquake.

Fran! Why won't they let me in to see her! While Jack had been away, Molly told him, a bed had been found for Fran in intensive care. She needed close observation, and the doctors said they'd prefer that Jack wait outside, at least for the next few hours. Of course, there was no space in the waiting room, so Jack was seated on a stacking chair in the hallway again. Fatigue was catching up with him. Despite the noise and activity, he was able to get some sleep, if only a little.

He was worried about Fran, especially since he knew she had been taken to intensive care. And he was tired and confused. He liked it when things were orderly, predictable, and well under control. The thing he found most difficult about ministry was his inability to control crises. He loved the weeks when everything went smoothly so he could complete all his work according to plan.

Those weeks were rare. Something was always happening. Somebody was always doing something stupid, and he, of course, got the call. He was the pastor, and that's the pastor's job. Only this time it wasn't someone else's problem. This was his wife's life and his problem, even without factoring in the uproar of the whole city and the fact that the church no longer had a building.

His thoughts were interrupted by a familiar voice coming from a room across the hall. Jack felt bold enough to poke his head inside the door. "Terri? Is that you?"

"Who's that?" said a voice from behind a partially pulled curtain.

"Jack Newman—Tom's brother."

"Jack," Terri Jones said with warmth. "Yes, please come in. Feel free."

Jack stepped around the curtain and found her looking a little disheveled, in an attractive way. "I must say, you look great . . . for a person in a hospital bed, I mean."

Unprofessional! Jack knew it right away. He'd never have said something like that if he were here on a pastoral call. He felt out of his element. He felt like a schoolboy. She really was good-looking. . . .

"So you're on your pastoral rounds?" Terri questioned. "I imagine you have a lot of people to see after something like this. It's nice that you found a moment for me."

"Actually, no," Jack said. "I was just waiting out in the hall. My wife is here, but they won't let me see her right now. I guess you could say I'm off duty." He smiled.

She shifted on the bed uncomfortably. The sheet slipped, revealing part of her right leg, bare to the thigh. Jack averted his gaze, but not until the image was well imprinted in his mind.

"What happened to you?" he asked.

"Dumb car accident."

"Car accident? The hospital is full of earthquake victims, and you had a car accident?" It could have been funny.

"I'm an earthquake victim too," she said. "I suppose that's how I ended up in a wreck." She told him about the damage to her building. "I'll be out of here later this evening, I'm sure. They wanted to check me out and make sure everything's in the right place. I don't think I'm very badly hurt. In fact, I'm feeling guilty about getting my own bed and everything with all the demand here today."

"They kept Fran out in the hall for a couple of hours."

"I'm more concerned about what will happen when I'm released. I can't go home. There is no home. Not anymore."

Jack didn't feel much like a pastor. His instincts were all wrong. Her eyes were exquisite, even in a hospital bed. He began to imagine what she'd look like dressed up, as if for dinner.

Terri began to cry. Jack had to look closely to notice it, but there was a tear. His head was swimming. He took her hand as if to console her. He intended the gesture to be pastoral. It wasn't.

He was physically excited. He was adrift.

⁂

Chloe Ellis returned with a glass bottle of iced tea and a sesame bagel. It wasn't so much that she was hungry as that she'd been looking for something to do. The convenience store three blocks away had offered a welcome retreat. The downside was that she'd lost her seat in the waiting room and everyone there looked well ensconced. She noticed an empty chair in the hallway and quickly sat down.

She took another bite of her bagel and set it down, using her hand-bag on her lap as a table. The door to the room across the hall was open. She could hear voices, one of which sounded like Jack Newman's. She entered the room without concern. Maybe he'd heard something about Fran. Maybe they'd moved her to this room.

Chloe saw Jack in close with a woman she didn't recognize. She saw him holding her hand. Pastors did that, she told herself. Pastors hold the hands of people they meet in hospitals—the healing touch, and all that. She was trying to convince herself. Pastors come to hospitals to care for people. That's what they call it—*pastoral care.* Chris did it all the time. The thought chilled her.

Stewart Rylie closed his cell phone, having left another message on Jack Newman's voice mail. Henry Ellis had told him about the destruction of the church building, and he'd just been there to see for himself. He couldn't remember anything like this happening before during his long tenure as the denomination's district supervisor. With Jack's wife in the hospital, the situation was a real problem. Jack was already in a fragile state, given what had been happening with his best friend, Chris Ellis. Maybe I should try to catch him at the hospital, he thought.

Jack was leaving the parking lot from the east exit just as Stewart was entering from the west. It was evening, and he was going home. Fran was improving. They'd let him in to see her, and she'd shown some sign of recognition. Still . . .

Entering the kitchen, he checked the refrigerator. It was habit. He wasn't even hungry. He closed the door and sat down on his couch with the lights off. Looking out the front window, he watched the cars go by and thought about Terri. He told himself that pure care and concern motivated his action, but he wasn't fool enough to believe that.

He rebuilt her image in his mind and indulged his guilty pleasure. She was homeless, certainly the most beautiful homeless person he'd ever come across. He should have invited her to stay with him. They had a guest room. Fran wasn't home, and Jack was hardly ever there himself, so there'd be room for her.

He went to bed and tried to sleep.

———

It was embarrassing. The desk clerk recognized Tom as a celebrity news anchor and was making a fuss over him. The fact that he was here with a beautiful woman without any luggage was discomforting. Tom pulled out his credit card. "Make it just a room for one," Tom said. "The young lady will be staying alone."

"I understand, completely," the clerk said, trying to sound helpful.

Did he wink at me? Tom couldn't be sure. The whole thing would have been humiliating, except for the fact that Terri needed a friend, and she needed a place to stay now that she had been released from the hospital. He didn't feel right, as her boss, about letting her stay at his home. They'd have to come up with another arrangement quickly, but for now, the hotel was the best option.

"I'll see you to the elevator door, but I'll let you tuck yourself in," Tom said.

They walked together across the hotel lobby. Terri had appreciated his help, and he was glad to offer it. It was funny how he was changing. When Terri had first come to work for him, he'd have killed to have this kind of opportunity. She was vulnerable. He was caring. It was a perfect opportunity to get more *intimately* acquainted. But now, he had no interest. Well, no, that wasn't it exactly. He hadn't lost interest. How could he? She was gorgeous and, well, he felt something for her. He just didn't want to take advantage of her. He wanted to do the right thing.

The thought was a welcome surprise.

———

Engage the Problem . . .

Jack couldn't sleep, even though he was exhausted. He lay there in bed with his eyes closed, trying to think heavy, sleepy thoughts, but he wasn't getting anywhere with it. He tried to pray. Sometimes when he couldn't sleep he'd try to get into prayer. Prayer often made him sleepy, which he knew wasn't a great motive for praying. But if it didn't work, at least he'd be using the time productively. Besides, it was still early.

He wanted to pray, but it felt awkward to him—dishonest somehow, and so he stopped trying. He thought about the church and felt drawn toward it. He tried to check the time, but it was dark and his watch wasn't glowing properly. He flicked the light switch, blinking back the drowsiness. He pulled a pair of sweatpants and a sweatshirt over his shorts and T-shirt and searched for his wallet and keys.

The site looked eerie in the moonlight. The church was located in an older business district, and everyone had gone home. No one was around. A wide strip of yellow and black tape circled the remains of what had recently been the house of the Lord.

Jack got out of the car and sat on the curb. He thought about his sermon.

"Yet once more shall I shake not only the earth, but also heaven."

Ominous! What had happened here? Jack wondered. *Did God do this as some act of judgment? If so, judgment for what?* Sure, we're all sinners, but this seemed a little too Old Testament. It was too beyond the ordinary, even for God. What was God saying?

Jack realized that his briefcase was on the backseat. He was fortunate that it wasn't lost in the wreckage. His sermon notes, such as they were, were still safe. Jack wasn't sure whether that was a good thing. He went to the car and retrieved the case. He pulled out his laptop, hoping he had enough battery power. He turned it on and called up the file.

This would be the third major move of his sermon—the third quadrant, as he'd come to call it, where the sermon tried to move from understanding to assent. It required honesty and humility. The sermon would have to be real to the preacher in order to be real for the listeners. "Engage the problem." Well that was real enough. There was plenty of problem for this sermon in this moment. He tried to focus on the notes he'd written earlier in the week.

God's kingdom can't be shaken. So long ago, it seemed, he'd written the second quadrant tagline, the answer to the question, "What's the point?" He had felt so confident, so assured. *It was a lot easier for me to say something like that a couple of days ago,* he admitted. *It's much harder to maintain that kind of confidence when the ground is shaking beneath my feet.*

He read the passage again to himself, slowly. God could really put a scare into people. The text talked about mountains touched with fire, darkness, gloom, and storm. It described the sound of trumpets and "such a voice speaking words that those who heard it begged that no further word be spoken to them" (Heb. 12:19). Even Moses was terrified. "I am trembling with fear," he said (v. 21). Sitting beside his collapsed church building, Jack found it easy to imagine the ancient Hebrews standing at the foot of Mount Sinai with smoke and flames billowing from the summit.

Engage the Problem

Moving from Understanding to Assent

▶ Once you've established the point, be honest about your own objections and assumptions.

▶ Give God's Spirit time and space to address the listener's reluctance.

▶ Be humble enough that people can sense you're telling them the truth.

But the text seems to say that it's different for us. As New Testament believers, we stand at a different location in salvation history. This is *not* what *we* have come to, the text said. "But you have come to Mount Zion, to the heavenly Jerusalem" (v. 22a). The passage described the city of the living God, with thousands of joy-singing angels. It described Jesus, the Mediator of a new covenant, who puts us on a different level than those beside the mountain with Moses. There is a hopeful tone to the text. Jack wondered if he could preach in that voice of optimism on Sunday.

Jack stood and began to pace. In the distance he could hear the traffic. But right here, right now, it was quiet. He really wanted to pray. He understood the high and mighty thing he was proposing to do. He felt underqualified. Worse, he felt wrong for the job—all wrong. Pictures of Fran and Chris and Terri were mixed up in his mind. He felt so confoundedly *human.*

The Fallen Condition Focus

Since God designed the Bible to complete us, its contents necessarily indicate that in some sense we are incomplete. Our lack of wholeness is a consequence of the fallen condition in which we live.

—Bryan Chapell

Maybe that was okay. He thought about what Bryan Chapell had said in his book about "The Fallen Condition Focus"—the concern to make every sermon speak to the reality of the human sin condition.[2] Right now, Jack felt, his fallen condition was all too focused.

On reflection, maybe it wasn't a bad stance from which to preach. Maybe this was exactly where he needed to be . . . exactly where God wanted him. Maybe God had put him in the place where he could preach this Sunday. Maybe this was what he needed to be able to preach this sermon. But it seemed an awful price.

Henry had drummed into his head the importance of spiritual preparation for preaching. Jack understood that a person who professes to lead the people of God into the presence of God must first have spent his own time with God. This was the moment, he knew. Right here. Right now. If he were to have any chance of helping people hear from God, then he would have to hear from God himself right now, in this place.

Jack climbed onto the pile of wreckage and tried to find the place where the pulpit would have stood. He paced twelve uneven steps from the spot where he thought he could detect the northern sanctuary wall.

Little was recognizable, but he took it on faith that he had the right spot. He managed to clear some ground in the rubble where he got down on his knees.

It came as a humbling—the sense of God's spirit. It wasn't dramatic. Winds didn't blow and fire didn't fall, yet Jack knew that God had visited him. *Was all this for me? Chris? The earthquake? Was it all to teach me about the power of God and my dependence upon him?*

No doubt there were many things God was doing for many people through the events of the past few days, Jack decided. For him, for now, it was a lesson in humility and a reminder of power. Anything good that comes from a sermon comes from God. It is God's pleasure to use weak people to proclaim his Word. We bear this treasure in jars made of clay, so God can be glorified in us as his purposes are fulfilled.

Jack stood up, sobered. "Use me," he prayed. It wasn't a long prayer. The language wasn't elaborate. It felt, in fact, that the prayer was expressed more in what he felt than in what he put into words. "Keep me from the evil in my heart," he said simply. "Make me someone you can use. Make my words your words. Don't let me miss this opportunity to help people hear what you have in mind."

———

Leaving several minutes later, Jack noticed a figure poking around in the debris. The person looked familiar, yet he was too far away to get a good look. Jack was tempted to leave him alone. He didn't want to have to deal with a looter, and there wasn't much in the way of loot to be had. On the other hand, maybe he was a parishioner. Maybe he needed help.

"Who's there?" Jack called. The figure turned, paused, and then turned again, departing abruptly. Jack caught his breath when he saw the person's face. It was Chris Ellis.

"Chris," Jack yelled. "Wait! Please, Chris, don't go. We need to talk. . . . Please, come back."

Jack hurried to the place where Chris had been and found what he had been looking at. It was the church's old wooden pulpit. The base had been crushed, but the top piece was still intact, the dedication nameplate still attached—scuffed, but still readable. Jack stared at the pulpit top for several minutes.

He had an idea.

4

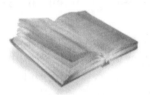

Fidelity

IMAGINE THE DIFFERENCE

It was late. Chloe Ellis was tired. She entered the hotel with her head down, fumbling in her purse for her room key.

Terri Jones was worn out as well. It was a fine mess, wasn't it? Tom Newman had seen her safely to the elevator door like a gentleman. She was lucky she could call on him. How many women had a boss like this? She shouldn't have let him go. She should have invited him upstairs. She could have insisted. The elevator hadn't left yet, but the door was closing. On impulse she threw her foot between the doors and pried them open.

"Tom," she yelled, running forward to catch him before he left.

The collision wasn't severe, but it was enough to cause Chloe to drop her key card, which landed on its edge and slid under a couch.

"I'm so sorry," Terri said, looking truly embarrassed.

Chloe recognized the voice first and then the face. It was the woman who'd been with Jack Newman at the hospital. She wasn't sure what to say, so she chose to say nothing. Instead, she got down on her knees and tried to get the card out from underneath the couch with her hand. It was no use, and the couch was heavy.

"Let me help you," Terri said putting her small frame against the piece of furniture as if to move it from its place. "Maybe we can get this thing to move."

"Is this what you're looking for?" Tom Newman said to Chloe, holding the key card in his hand. "It must have slid all the way through to the other side."

Now it was Chloe's turn to feel embarrassed. She recognized him immediately. These Newmans were everywhere!

"Again, let me say I'm sorry," Terri said.

Chloe was starting to think she really meant it. "I'm sorry too, I wasn't looking where I was going."

"No harm done," Terri said. "Look," she said to Tom, her resolve broken, "I'll call you in the morning."

"What did you want?" Tom asked.

"Nothing. You get some sleep." Terri quickly moved toward the elevator and disappeared from sight.

Tom turned his attention to the familiar looking woman in front of him. "I know you, don't I?" he asked.

"Not really," Chloe said. "I'm married to your brother's best friend. Chloe Ellis," she said, extending her hand.

"Of course," Tom acknowledged. "Jack talks about you. He's very fond of you and your husband."

"Chris and Jack go back a long way."

Tom didn't say anything directly in response. He was beginning to feel a mild embarrassment. He felt a need to explain his presence. "I was just dropping my assistant here at the hotel. The earthquake left her homeless, I'm afraid."

"I think I saw her at the hospital today."

"Yes," Tom said, "she was there for several hours. She's fine, of course, but they were taking precautions."

"I saw her there with Jack," Chloe said awkwardly.

The way she said it caught him off guard. "Why were you at the hospital? I hope you're all right."

"I'm fine. I was there with Fran."

"Fran?" Tom showed his surprise.

"You hadn't heard?" Clearly he hadn't, from the look on his face. "She was injured in the earthquake."

"No." Tom was shaken. "How is she? I didn't know. I haven't spoken to Jack since the earthquake struck. We were together when it happened, but since then we've both been going so hard we haven't connected. I hadn't heard about Fran."

"I think she's going to be fine," Chloe answered. "That's why I've come back. I didn't want to leave her until the doctors could assure me that things would be all right."

"Come back?" Tom asked. "This is a hotel."

He doesn't miss much, Chloe thought. "That's another story. Maybe some other time."

Tom wasn't sure how to respond to that one. "You said that Jack was with Terri. She didn't say anything about seeing him there."

"I'm sure she didn't," Chloe said, a tinge of bitterness in her voice. She regretted the words as soon as they were spoken.

"What do you mean?"

Chloe didn't say anything—not at first. She didn't want to say anything at all. She just wanted to return to her room and go to bed. Except that Tom Newman wasn't leaving. He just kept looking at her with his inquiring newsman eyes. "They seemed a little chummy," she said.

With that, she gathered herself and made her escape. "I'm sorry," she said. "I'm sure I didn't mean what I said, or didn't see what I thought. I didn't think. That's it." The elevator door was open. She quickly pushed the "close door" button and looked at herself in the mirror. Unwelcome tears were rolling down her cheeks.

"Jack, it's Stewart Rylie."

"Hello, Stewart." Jack was on his cell phone on his way home from the church.

"I'm sorry to call so late at night. I've been trying to reach you all day. There was no answer at your home, so I figured you were still out."

"It's not a problem," Jack said. "You can call me anytime." He meant what he said. "I was just returning from the church, or what's left of it."

"You've had quite a week."

"I suppose I have, and I'm not sure it's over."

"Listen, Jack, I'm returning from a late board meeting and my wife's out of town. I'm not too far away from your place right now. Do you want to sit down and talk?"

The two agreed to meet at a nearby all-night donut shop, the kind of place where they let you sit all night for the price of a cup of coffee and a donut. Jack, of course, ordered a cola.

"You can drink that stuff this time of night?" Stewart joked. "It'd keep me awake."

"You mean unlike that jumbo coffee you're drinking?" Jack answered. "How many of those have you had today?"

Stewart let the comment pass. "How's Fran?" he asked.

"You know, I think she's going to be fine. I was worried for a while. They couldn't seem to tell me whether it was serious or not. She took a nasty blow to the head, then with the sedation and all, I think she just took the opportunity to get caught up on her sleep."

"I'm glad to hear it, Jack. She'll be back home tomorrow?"

"I don't know the plan yet. She spoke to me tonight briefly, and I could barely understand her. She seemed so weak but at least she spoke. The doctor seems to think it was a good sign. They've been doing tests and so far she seems to be passing them."

"That's great news—the best news. It really is. You're going to have enough to deal with at the church over the next little while."

"It is a terrible mess."

"We can sort that out tomorrow. Your insurance was paid up, wasn't it?"

"Sure, we're up to date on the premiums."

"Good," Stewart said. "I've got some ideas about what we can do in the meantime. Maybe we can talk about it in the morning."

"I've got some ideas about it myself," Jack said.

The two men sat quietly for a few minutes. Then Jack spoke again.

"Stewart," he said. There was a fresh intensity on his face, as if he'd only now resolved to bring up something critical. "How honest am I allowed to be?"

"With me?" Stewart said. "I can keep a confidence. Of course, if it's . . ."

"No, no," Jack said, "not with you. I'm talking about with my congregation. How honest can I be in my preaching?"

Stewart didn't answer right away.

"I was always taught that the preacher ought to keep himself out of the way of the sermon. My old homiletics teachers used to teach that the preacher shouldn't say a lot about himself in the pulpit. We were supposed to get out of the way of the text so God could speak without us impeding his purposes," Jack said.

Negatives: Human Preachers . . .

- ▶ misinterpret the message
- ▶ compete with the message
- ▶ tarnish the message

"I understand that kind of thinking," Stewart said. "Human beings don't seem up to the task of representing God's Word. Give us a chance and we will misinterpret the message, let our egos compete with the message, or sometimes even tarnish the message by the way we're living. It can't be avoided. We're not robots. We're human, and this is what happens when we let humans preach."

"Sounds like you have been thinking about this," Jack said.

"You're right," Stewart said. "I just gave you the outline of a presentation I'm working on for a pastor's conference next month."

"That's great. Lay it on me."

Stewart smiled. "I never turn down an audience," he said. "What we're talking about here is the humanity of the preacher, and there are two ways of thinking about the subject. On the one hand, we can view the preacher's humanity as a negative. If that's how we see it, we'll try to *repress* our human nature."

"And if we chose to view it positively?"

"Then we'll *express* our humanity," Stewart said. "There are at least three things that can be said on each side of the argument. Negatively, as I already mentioned, preachers can do terrible things to a text, precisely because we are human."

"I don't see how we can help it," Jack said. "We read the text from within our human framework. We're bound to treat it subjectively."

"That's one problem," Stewart agreed. "The second is that we'll compete with the message God wants preached. The preacher who tells a personal story runs the risk of either looking too good or looking too bad. In the former case, he can appear arrogant and self-serving. In the latter case, he risks the negation of either his point or his authority by describing too much difficulty in living up to the demands of the text. In both cases, the preacher draws attention to himself at the expense of the text."

"I've always found that the very position of the preacher is seductive." Jack said. "Just standing up in front of a crowd like that is a powerful place to be. You can find yourself encouraging the personal attention, just by the way you dress or the way you carry yourself.

"When listeners pay more attention to the preacher than to the sermon, the whole process has been sabotaged."

"But there's more," said Stewart. "The worst problem with the preacher's humanity is that we're so messed up. Every preacher I've ever met is a dirty rotten sinner."

"The public would agree with you, that's for sure," said Jack. "Every poll I have seen that measures public trust in various occupational groups rates preachers near the bottom of the pile."

"All have sinned, and have fallen short of the glory of God."

"You want to see my feet of clay?" Jack joked.

"I don't need to, Jack. They're obvious to everyone who knows you."

Jack wasn't sure if he should take offense.

"Don't worry," Stewart continued, "It's true of all of us. We all depend on God's grace for the right and the power to preach. We just don't want to get too comfortable with that fact."

The discussion was more than hypothetical to Jack. He took another bite of his donut. "You said there is a positive side to this?"

Positives: Human Preachers . . .

- ▶ real-ize the message
- ▶ reckon with the message
- ▶ endorse the message

"Sure," Stewart said. "One of the things I like best about preaching is that I can *real*-ize the text for the people. One of the difficulties inherent in preaching is the otherworldliness of the message. Here we are, trying to offer transcendent truth to people who can't escape their own location within space and time. How can the finite appreciate the infinite? How can the contemporary listener overcome his or her subjective nature sufficiently to gain access to the objective? Somehow he or she has to perceive the message as real. Speaking of the text in real terms, offering contemporary examples and real human interaction, makes the truth more accessible."

"I can relate to that," Jack said. "Lofty ideas can sound very ordinary coming out of my mouth."

"Not ordinary, Jack," Stewart said, "but real, alive, and relevant. At least you have a chance of winning a hearing if you can come off looking real. Fred Craddock says that 'the distance between ourselves and the original readers of the text is bridged by our common humanity.'[1] Maybe we ought to use that in our favor. Maybe we can help our listeners appreciate the text as something real if we present it as something real from our own life and experience."

"I like that," Jack said.

"Of course, if we're going to *real*-ize the message, we're going to have to *reckon* with the message."

"What do you mean?"

"Haddon Robinson said biblical preaching is when the Holy Spirit takes a biblical concept and applies it, first to the preacher, then through him to his hearers.[2] If you want your listeners to take the sermon seriously, then you have to take it seriously yourself in real terms in real time. It has to matter to you before it can matter to them."

"I remember Henry Ellis telling me the same thing. Listeners need to hear more of this kind of thing in our preaching."

"That's the third positive," Stewart said, "Preachers who are willing to describe their own experience with the text *endorse* the message of the text. A preacher who has earned the trust of the congregation can greatly enhance the impact of the message through the telling of a few well chosen personal stories."

"I always felt that, by endorsing the message through my own life experience and stories, I'm somehow able to bear some of the burden of authority for the message, not in opposition to the Bible's inherent authority but in concert with it."

"The problem with trying to repress your humanity in preaching," Stewart said, "is that it's impossible. You can no more renounce your humanity than you can grow gills and swim like a fish."

Jack smiled at the mental image of a tuna in the pulpit.

"Sometimes," Stewart continued, "I think we're uncomfortable in our own skin. We misunderstand our own impulses. We doubt ourselves. It's frustrating, bewildering, and exhilarating, and it's all part of God's plan."

"Not only is it impossible to put off our humanity," Jack added, "but it's unnecessary."

"The Incarnation ought to have taught us that," Stewart agreed.

"Jesus perfectly presented the Word through the medium of flesh, but then," Jack said, "he is Jesus."

"And you're not, right?"

"You have no idea."

Stewart paused, wondering if Jack was going to reveal something.

For just a moment, Jack almost did. His sudden feelings of sexual desire for Terri Jones had shaken him. That he could entertain such thoughts, especially with his wife in a hospital bed nearby, awakened him to the depth of his own depravity. He could never speak of it. His people could never know. Surely, there was a limit to what a pastor could say from the pulpit, wasn't there? "You still haven't answered my question, Stewart."

"What question?"

"How honest can I be when I'm preaching?" The conversation had gained intensity. Jack was looking firmly into Stewart's eyes.

Stewart answered his friend directly. "You have to be careful, Jack.

I've seen pastors bleed all over the pulpit. I've seen them use the pulpit as a kind of psychiatrist's couch, looking for some kind of catharsis through self-exposure. I've seen good people lose their jobs because they've lost the people's trust."

Jack was thinking about Chris Ellis.

"You don't have to be the people's hero. In fact, if you're the hero of every story you tell, that'll get old in a real hurry. Know your people. Know your limits. Be real with them, but not so real that they'll want to take your job away from you."

Stewart was being blunt, and Jack appreciated it.

"What if you deserve to have your job taken away from you?"

"Jack," Stewart's head was tilted a few degrees to the left. "You don't have anything to confess, do you?"

There was a long silence as Jack thought about that. He didn't believe he'd crossed the line—although he certainly had gotten close enough to it to measure its dimensions.

He stood up and took out his wallet. He pulled out a twenty-dollar bill and left it on the table. It was far too much. "Take that for my part of the donuts and keep the rest for your counseling fee," he said, as he moved to walk away. He stopped and turned. "Don't worry, Stewart, I'm fine." He turned to leave again before stopping once more. "Thank you, Stew. I mean it. This has been helpful. I'll call you in the morning about arrangements for the church. As I said, I've got a plan."

The message light was blinking when Jack returned home. "Jack, phone me; doesn't matter how late. Call me when you get in."

"Tom," Jack said moments later. "I've been meaning to talk to you."

"I just heard about Fran. Are you all right, buddy? I hear she's going to be okay."

"It looks that way," Jack answered. "I'm very relieved. God has been good."

Tom smiled, not in the wry, sarcastic way he used to smile whenever Jack worked God into the conversation. This was a knowing smile, a smile of recognition. "He has," Tom agreed, "but really, Jack, I want to make sure you're holding up. I mean, with the church and everything."

"Yeah, I'm doing great. I just had a long talk with a good friend. Sorted a few things out, you know. As the old hymn says, 'It is well with my soul.'"

Tom wasn't up on his old hymns. He changed the subject. "I heard you met Terri." He didn't mean to accuse his brother, but it was hard to keep the tone out of the statement.

Jack felt himself blushing. He paused to compose himself. "She's a great young woman. You're blessed to have her working for you. And really, Tom, I'm fine."

"Glad to hear it," Tom was relieved. He believed his brother.

"By the way," Jack asked, "what's the forecast for Sunday? What's your weatherman saying?"

"Why do you ask?"

⊷⊶⊷

Terri Jones was at her desk earlier than normal. After the events of the day before, she felt a need to show that she was back in the saddle. Tom Newman had shaken his head when he came in and saw her already there. Terri only smiled as they began the daily briefing.

"I've got a special story I'd like to pursue," Tom said.

"What is it, Tom?"

"It's my brother." That got Terri's attention. "His church, actually— kind of a 'feel good' story in the aftermath of the earthquake. I think I'm going to take a full crew out there this afternoon."

"You're the boss."

⊷⊶⊷

Henry Ellis paused to stretch, a huge grin on his face. His back was sore, but it didn't matter to him.

"This is a little more challenging than setting up chairs," Jack was wearing his own smile.

"We've still got to put out chairs. There's not much left of the pews." Henry held up a scrap of thick wood that had seen service as the sidepiece of a church pew bench, the carved cross still visible in the varnished pine.

"I've got chairs coming tomorrow morning," Jack said. "Stewart Rylie said he'd take care of it for us."

"I hope he brings a lot of them. My guess is that we're going to have a great crowd."

"Anna's working the phones pretty hard, I hear."

Henry grinned. Anna had jumped at the opportunity to do something useful—anything to take her mind off the situation with Chris.

Jack and Henry and several others were knee-deep in rubble when Jack thought he felt the ground shift. "Did you feel that?" Jack asked, his worry undisguised.

"I felt something," Henry said. "I think the pile shifted a little."

"Not another aftershock?"

Henry wasn't sure if the movement had been imagined or whether it was caused by a heavy truck that was coming around the corner. The truck, bearing the logo of *Eye-Witness News*, was setting up alongside the church property. A camera crew was climbing out of the truck, unloading equipment and looking for places to set up. Tom Newman, well dressed as usual, climbed out of the front seat, microphone in hand.

"Is the light okay?" Tom asked.

An assistant gave him the thumbs-up.

"The city is starting to rebuild after the trauma of this week's earthquake," Tom was saying. "Anyone looking for a source of inspiration could do no better than to look here at the corner of Fiftieth Avenue and Oak Street. Three days ago, this site featured one of our city's most historic churches. Three stories high, it's been helping people find inspiration for more than one hundred years. The earthquake reduced the church to rubble earlier this week, but it hasn't destroyed the faith of these willing volunteers. This Sunday, people will find a new kind of encouragement in the services performed by . . . well . . . by my brother, Pastor Jackson Newman."

Chris Ellis was back home when he turned on his television. He couldn't see the sense in Chloe and him both staying in hotels. Besides, she'd have to come back eventually, and then they could talk. He was ready to talk, he felt. He had to talk to someone.

That's Jack, he said to himself, as the image of his friend was featured on the television news. Chris watched the report, a piece of warmed-up pizza from the fridge growing cold in his hand. Something stirred as he saw pictures of his father helping others clear the grounds so there'd be room for people to come and worship on Sunday morning.

Dad has been great, Chris thought. I can't imagine how disappointed he must be with me, when all he did was love me. He listened to the hopeful words Jack was saying to his brother Tom on camera, and he felt the tears begin to flow.

He picked up the phone and called the hotel. He didn't have to look up the number. He had it memorized though he'd never used it. He had intended to, but had never been able to find the courage, until now. "Pick up," he said. "Please, Chloe, pick up the phone."

"The occupant of the room you have dialed is not available. Please leave a message on the hotel's automated voice mail system." Chris replaced the phone in the cradle, wondering whom else he might be able to call.

⸺⸺⸺

Imagine the Difference . . .

"I'm really grateful you were willing to meet with me." Chris Ellis looked down. "After the way I treated you when you came to visit at the hotel. . . ."

"It's better this way," Jack answered. "I'm not sure either of us would have appreciated what I came to say that night."

"It's great what you're doing here," Chris said, pointing at the church grounds. The two were sitting in the front seat of Jack's ancient Impala. The church property had adopted a surreal look in the moonlight. A makeshift platform had been established. Remnants of the old pulpit had been fashioned together to serve for one more sermon. All that was needed was the chairs.

"I think I saw you here the other night."

"You did," Chris admitted. "I came looking for you—or looking for God. But when I saw you, I couldn't bring myself to actually talk to you."

"You were reaching out."

"I was scared." Chris was starting to cry, which was beginning to feel like his normal state. "I'm going to come and hear you preach tomorrow. And it had better be a good one." He tried to smile. "I'm going to need some special kind of preaching to get me through this. You're going to have to be amazing."

"I'm sure I'll disappoint you on that one," Jack said. "But that's all right. You don't need me to be amazing. You need God to be amazing, and that's a good thing for you, because he is always amazing, more than you or I have ever imagined. I'm just the messenger boy, just the one who gets to tell everyone about it." Jack stopped, embarrassed by his enthusiasm. He wasn't saying anything Chris didn't know himself. Chris had been in this line of work as long as he had.

"I don't know how many sermons I've preached since seminary," Chris said. "In the beginning, I had such a big vision for what we were doing. Preaching seemed so powerful. It seemed so important. After a while, I guess I grew cold. I forgot what my calling was about. My preaching shriveled. My vision shrunk. I couldn't imagine what difference my preaching could make."

"Funny you should say it that way," Jack said. "You couldn't 'imagine the difference.' That's the way I'd put it, too. I'm now rewriting that phrase as a critical signpost over my preaching: 'Imagine the Difference.' I use it to help me think about the final move of the sermon. My task . . ." Jack paused. "I'm sorry I got carried away. I don't imagine you want to be talking about . . ."

"No," Chris jumped in quickly. "It helps to talk about preaching. Better that than dwelling on the other stuff."

The other stuff. Jack would have loved to talk about the other stuff. He had so many questions about it. Why he did it. . . . Why did she . . . ?

No—much better to talk about preaching. There'd be a time for the other stuff.

"My task," Jack continued, "as I come to close out my sermon, is to use my imagination to try to envision how the message God has given me could change everything. Rather than just trying to wrap things neatly, I'm trying to find what I could say that would break things loose and get everybody motivated. There's so much at stake in our preaching. I want to help people see what could be if we really listened to the voice of God and did the things he says. I'm becoming convinced that there's no point preaching if we don't expect to see a difference."

The two men paused as a police car sped through the intersection, its lights flashing.

Imagine the Difference

What would it look like if the sermon worked—if people actually heard from God and responded the way he expected them to?
- ▶ Determine the mood the sermon requires.
- ▶ Discern the active response the sermon would expect— sermons should always make a difference.
- ▶ Examine the intent of the sermon from various human perspectives.

"I try," Jack said, "to ask the question, 'What would it look like, smell like, taste like, feel like, if people actually responded to the message God was offering?' What would happen? What would change? I try to let my imagination soar, to think big, practical, important thoughts about what God could do if we would only listen and respond."

"How do you motivate that kind of change?" Chris was starting to remember the preacher within him.

"It's more than just addressing the listener's mind," Jack said. "That's for sure. I've got to motivate them. I have to speak to their hearts, tell their stories, offer hope, get passionate about the whole thing."

Jack paused to think.

"Years ago I read Jonathan Edwards' work on religious affections.

He wrote about those intangible things that motivate action in the believer—things like love or hate, desire, hope, fear. I remember he wrote, 'I am bold to assert, that there never was any considerable change wrought in the mind or conversation of any person, by anything of a religious nature, that ever he read, heard or saw, that had not his affections moved.'³ Something like that." Jack was surprised he remembered the quote so well.

"So how do you touch those kinds of things in preaching?" Chris really wanted to know.

"You dream dreams. You paint pictures. You kick some congregational . . . well, you know what you kick. You stir the juices. Most of all, you anticipate the presence of the Holy Spirit, and you observe the presence of God in the place. You inspire the people with the possibility of a revisioned future, and you connect them with the God who is present to help them see that vision fulfilled in their lives."

"I'd like to hear that kind of preaching just about now," Chris said.

"Show up tomorrow, and you just might."

It sounded almost arrogant, but both men understood the spirit in which it was intended.

"What happened to you, Chris?" Jack wasn't sure he could ask the question, until he realized he couldn't not ask it.

"I dunno. It didn't happen all at once. I don't know enough psychology to understand all the underlying reasons. All I know is that I let down the guard around my private life."

Jack nodded, trying to encourage more.

"The Internet didn't help. It started innocently enough. It usually does, I guess. Swimsuit models and eventually I graduated to something a little more titillating. I honestly don't know how I was able to continue to preach. Eventually, pictures of women on the Internet weren't enough. I began looking at women in a way I never had before." Chris was sobbing now.

"You should have told me," Jack said.

"Of course I should have told you," Chris agreed.

"I'd have been there for you."

"I know you would have been. It might even have made the difference."

"You remember the story of Moses in the battle with the Amalekites in Exodus 17? Moses stood on a hill overlooking the battlefield with his staff. As long as he held up his arms, Israel did well in battle, but as soon as he let his arms down, they began to lose ground."

"But his arms got tired," Chris said.

"He was, of course, only human. You can imagine how tired he must have felt, and yet how he wanted to keep holding his hands up."

"Thank the Lord that Moses had friends," said Chris.

"I'll bet he was thankful when Aaron and Hur came along to support his arms. Side by side they held up Moses' arms until the fighting ended. It's a great picture of friendship, brothers supporting each other in times of weariness."

"I know you would have tried, but I doubt I'd have let you be my support," Chris said. "I was in denial and didn't think I needed support. Asking for it would feel like an admission that I was doing something wrong. I'm not sure I'd have been up to that."

"So, can I hold your arms up now, Chris?" Jack asked. "I want to be there when you need me. I want you to know you can always tell me what you need—that you can always share your troubles with me. I'll be there, Chris. You know I will. I'll absolutely be there for you."

"I know you will," Chris said.

Jack let the moment sink in before speaking.

"Do you know what kind of a difference I'm imagining for tomorrow's sermon?" Jack asked. "Do you know what possibility I have in my mind?"

"Tell me."

"I'm praying that God will do something very special with you and Chloe, together. I anticipate seeing you praying together and sharing your lives together. I see you loving each other and loving God all over again."

All was silent. There was no traffic. The moment was holy.

"I *would* like to think that could happen," Chris Ellis said. "I'd like that very much."

Pastor Jack Newman pulled back the curtains and breathed a sigh of relief. It would be a fine morning. There wasn't a cloud to be seen. He showered and changed quickly. He'd risen early to spend time in prayer before people arrived.

He loved early Sunday morning. There was an edge to it, a little bit of nervousness, but mostly there was anticipation—a healthy sense of expectation. This Sunday morning his expectation was finely tuned. He was ready to preach. It would be one of those Sundays where it would be hard for him to sing the songs and read the announcements. *Just sit down, already, and let me preach!* . . . It would be a memorable service.

His preservice prayer was interrupted as people began to arrive, earlier than usual. The chairs were filling a full half-hour before the service was to begin. Stewart Rylie had been as good as his word. He'd arranged for a crew from another church to set up chairs on the church lawn, arrayed neatly around the wreckage that had been their church. Jack was beginning to wonder whether there'd be enough chairs.

There weren't. Fueled by Tom Newman's broadcast and Anna Ellis's phone blitz, and perhaps by the trauma of the earthquake itself, people gathered by the hundreds, more than Jack could ever remember for a service. Besides the regulars, he recognized others he knew from outside the church context. The guy who changed the oil in his car was there. So was a woman who frequently checked his groceries at the supermarket. Many other faces weren't familiar at all.

The service itself was simple. Electrical power was brought in from the office building next door to power the portable sound system so the worship team could be heard. That had been more difficult than anyone had thought. They had to pay the building's janitor for four hours just to unlock the door and plug in the cord. Maybe it'd be all right. He'd also hear the service.

Jack had worried that the traffic driving by and the chill in the air might have been distracting for people worshiping outdoors. In fact, the congregation seemed particularly well focused. There was a determination to their worship—as if they were declaring to themselves, to their God, and to the world that no disaster would dissuade them from their calling. Tissue could be seen dabbing the eyes of many a congregant. Some newcomers were visibly unfamiliar with the ways of a church service and seemed a bit uncomfortable, yet they were engaged and interested in what was happening around them.

Hebrews 12:28–29

Therefore, since we are receiving a kingdom that cannot be shaken, let us be thankful, and so worship God acceptably with reverence and awe, for our "God is a consuming fire."

Jack was especially pleased to see Chris sitting in the third row from the back on the far left side, trying to remain inconspicuous. Knowing Chris, this was likely the first time he hadn't preached on a Sunday since his vacation almost one year ago.

The crowd seemed hushed as Jack rose to speak. He began with very little preamble. He simply welcomed the newcomers and thanked the people for their willingness to worship outdoors. Then, in a strong voice, he read his text. He wanted to communicate his confidence that God was at work in their worship there that Sunday. His reading culminated in the powerful words of Hebrew 12:28–29, "Therefore, since we are receiving a kingdom that cannot be shaken, let us be thankful, and so worship God acceptably with reverence and awe, for our 'God is a consuming fire.'" With that, he prayed a simple prayer, asking that God would speak and that the people together would be willing to listen and to respond. Then he began.

Things have been a little shaky around here lately.

He tried to deliver his opening tagline in a lighthearted manner. A few people chuckled. A few others seemed unsure of whether chuckling was appropriate in a church.

It's been quite a week, hasn't it?

Many people nodded their agreement, Kathy Carswell among them. Jens Nilsson was sitting with his four teenage children. Jack couldn't tell for sure, but he looked like he might have been tearing up already. Molly Shires gave Jack an encouraging smile.

We live our lives in the knowledge that nothing is for sure, and that everything could change in the blink of an eye, but I'm not sure how much we really believe it until something like this happens. In a moment, in two shakes of the earth's crust, we come face to face with the fact that the whole thing is fragile. Everything could come crashing down around our ears in an instant.

Jack let that sit for a moment.

You know, I used to think that earthquake coverage is expensive. But now, looking around here, I realize it was money well spent. We have insurance, and we will rebuild this place.

The people burst into applause. One person even yelled his approval. A "more spiritual" soul shouted, "Amen!"

But I'm not sure we'll ever be the same again. We'll always know something of our frailty. Whenever a train comes by, or a heavy truck, and we feel the earth shake, we'll wonder, won't we?

You know the ancient Hebrew people faced similar circumstances. Hebrews 12 reminds us of a time when they met with God at the foot of Mount Sinai and the sound of his voice shook the very earth. Rocks tumbled and fire went up to heaven. But that wasn't the worst of it. They knew this was only the beginning—that one day God would speak again and this time his voice would shake not only the earth but also the heavens (v. 26). It's called judgment, and though the time has passed, we're still waiting with the memory, knowing the judgment of God is still there to be contended with. This world is accountable to the God who created it. One day it will all come tumbling down.

It was a strong message. Jack intended it to be. He was able to connect the story of the text (*their story*: the Hebrew memory of God's voice shaking the earth), with the listener's story (*our story*: the earthquake that happened just this week), with God's ultimate story (*his story*: impending judgment). No doubt he had the people's attention. What he did with it now would be the critical thing. Time to "make the point," Jack told himself.

God's kingdom can't be shaken. That's the good news I want you to hear this morning. In a world when everything is shaky, when everything is unstable, there's one safe place, one reliable thing that will not be shaken and that cannot fall down, the kingdom of God.

Jack read again the pivotal phrase in verse 28, "we are receiving a kingdom that cannot be shaken." He went back to verse 27, describing the image of temporal, created things having been removed, so that only the eternal remained.

I remember a Science World exhibit I went to several years ago. One room featured a major display of toys built out of Legos. Now, it's been a long time since I played with Lego blocks, but I was attracted enough to have a look around. The creativity and ingenuity of people are wonderful. There were racecars and animals and whole cities built out of Legos. One piece I was particularly taken with was a small earthquake simulator where people were encouraged to build a structure on a metal plate. Having built your building you would push a button to shake the whole thing. Bits and pieces would break off and fall away. The idea was to see whether you could build something strong enough to withstand the shaking.

I thought about that image when I read this text. There's only one thing in this world that can stand up to the kind of shaking we're talking about—only one thing that can stand up to judgment—and that is the kingdom of God.

He paused and wiped his forehead with a handkerchief. He felt as if he were sweating, even though the air was too cool to permit much in the way of perspiration.

When God stands up and speaks judgment to the world, there won't be much we can do. Everything impure and everything impermanent, everything weak and everything evil—it will all break off and fall away, ending up in a pile of dust and rubble on the ground. Only one thing will still stand, the unshakeable kingdom of God. And we'll be saved as long as we're attached to it. God's kingdom cannot be shaken.

It was a hopeful word. Jack wanted the people to catch the sense of promise inherent in the words, but not until they'd struggled with it for a time. Like an angler, he had his fish hooked, but he needed to let the fish run for a while before he tried to reel it in.

Of course it's hard to get a grip when the ground is shaking. It's hard to find the handles when the whole world seems unstable. *It's hard to find your footing when the ground is shaking underneath.*

There's an old story, written years ago by Joseph Addison. In it, he tells of an entrepreneur who finds himself on a tropical island. He does a booming business selling a pill that's, quote, 'very good against an earthquake.' Folks, I'd like to get me some of those pills. I could have used a boatload of them this week.[4]

Jack began to feel himself losing it just a little. As confident as he was trying to be, the week had shaken him deeply. He wanted to be strong for the people, but he was only human. He had feelings too. He paused and caught the eye of Pastor Henry who had taken a seat beside his son. Henry nodded and Jack moved forward with what he had come to say.

It has been an excruciating week for me, and frankly, the collapse of the church building was a very small part of what God has been taking me through. I've seen the collapse of relationships. I've seen my wife in the hospital. I've seen the weakness of good friends, and I've seen my own weakness in ways you probably wouldn't want to hear me talk about.

Some of the people squirmed as Jack continued, describing with care the trauma that comes when we struggle to be faithful in a world that feels so frail. Now Jack gave a little lift to his voice.

And yet, I've also seen God's grace. I've felt his forgiveness, and I've seen you, the body of Christ, show a resilience that proves the truth of our text.

Time to conclude, Jack told himself. He looked at Chris Ellis sitting in the crowd. He recalled their conversation from the previous evening. The pause was a little too long, but he needed to gather himself. He heard a stirring to the side and his eyes filled as he saw Chloe Ellis wheeling his wife, Fran, through the crowd.

Fran looked up at her husband and smiled. She held her hand up and waved at him. Their eyes met and Jack found himself unable to speak. Tom Newman stood up and went to Fran to hug her. By now the whole congregation had noticed and the meeting seemed at peril of breaking up in a relieved and joyful greeting. Jack was tempted to wrap it up right there, but he caught himself. What he was saying was too important. He had to bring this home.

We find our footing in the kingdom of God. Look at us here. Look at what we're doing here today. We didn't need this building in order to be the church. We didn't need the structure to give us viability. Theologians have told us for years that the church is not a building. The church is us—God's people. We are the church and here we are gathered together, as strong as ever, testimony to the fact.

Jack moved around to the side of the makeshift pulpit.

Take this pulpit . . . *please*. It doesn't look like much any-more. We used to take a certain pride in our furnishings, in our history, and in our structures. But we've learned that the whole thing can come crashing down and left in tatters, just like this pulpit.

Only one thing won't be shaken down. The kingdom is that one thing that will endure across time. It is the one thing that gives us hope. God's kingdom will never fall, and we will find our salvation in our attachment to that kingdom through the gracious sacrifice of our Lord Jesus Christ.

It was good, Jack thought, but not good enough. *Get specific*, he told himself.

Some of you are worried about your futures. You don't know if you can keep your job. You don't know if you can keep your faith. Hang on! Stay the course. God has a purpose, and he will see it through.

It felt good to offer hope. He remembered reading somewhere that if a preacher couldn't offer hope, he should sit down and shut his mouth. If a preacher didn't have hope, he didn't have anything.

Some of you might be hearing this for the first time—or for the first time in a long while. You want to believe that in these uncertain times there is a future, there is a trajectory to life, that this world is moving toward something, that there *is* hope for our futures. I'm here to tell you that hope exists and that it's found in Jesus Christ. It's available to any of you here. It's available to you today.

They were all gathered before him, the people who meant every-thing to him. These were the people he cared about, the ones over whom God had given him charge. He could have taken them one by one and described their life situations. He could have exhorted them individually, and in the days to come he probably would. For now, he spoke broadly, though directly. He spoke truth as one who loved them.

> We're receiving a kingdom that cannot be shaken. There is only one response and that response is worship. We must serve God. We must worship him in gratitude for the fact that he has assured our future. We will not be shaken as long as we're attached to the one reliable thing—the kingdom that cannot fall. Though all the earth comes crashing down around our ears, we will not fall. We will not be shaken. We are citizens of the kingdom—the unshakeable kingdom of God.

⸺⸱⸺

"They'll be talking about this Sunday for years to come," Tom Newman said afterward.

"I don't know," Jack said. "I'm not sure if I really got through. I wanted so much for this sermon. There was so much I wanted to say, and I just don't know if I did the message justice."

"I know the feeling." Henry Ellis had joined them on the lawn outside the church, and now he joined in. "I think I felt that way every time I preached."

"It got through to me," Tom Newman smiled. There was something about his smile. . . .

Jack examined his brother carefully. "What are you trying to say, Tom?" he asked.

Tom paused before responding. He was picking at something in the grass with the toe of his well-shined loafers. Eventually he looked up, a peaceful smile on his face. "I'm saying it's about time I found my footing. We need to meet, Jack. Maybe you could teach me how to pray."

Jack responded with a bear hug.

He would have kept hugging indefinitely if it weren't for the fact that there were others present. Chris and Chloe were talking, and that was a start. Henry had rejoined Anna in their seats. Anna was crying, but Jack felt sure these tears were different from the ones she'd been shedding earlier in the week.

Then there was Fran. Jack was anxious to show his wife just how much he loved her. There'd be time for that, in between reconstructing a building, counseling friends back to marital health, and preaching sermons, of course. It wouldn't be easy. He was, after all, only human. But, by God's grace and for his glory, he *would* persevere.

Jack returned to the platform and retrieved his Bible. Pausing before leaving, he stooped and picked up a piece of brick. He examined it, turning it over carefully in his fingers. He put it in his pocket and looked up to find his wife still smiling warmly at him. Jack smiled back and climbed down from the platform.

He had a sermon to live up to.

PART 2

Teaching

5

Clinic in Integrative Preaching

What has surprised me more than anything else since the publication of *Preaching with Conviction* is the response my preaching receives from senior believers. Having invested my energy in the development of a model for preaching to postmoderns, I shouldn't expect a constant flow of little old men and littler old ladies coming to express appreciation.

It happens, I think, because I give them the Bible. No matter what I'm trying to do, and no matter how creatively I'm trying to do it, I always want people to know that I'm giving them the Scriptures. That, after all, is where the power is. Many older saints recognize and appreciate this when they hear it.

I've come to think that we've become embarrassed by the Bible. At least you'd think so by attending many of our churches. It no longer seems important to carry a Bible to church. We keep our public readings brief, and we're sure to use the most contemporary paraphrase. The sermons themselves are heavy on the application, focusing on contemporary stories and metaphors, offering reference to the Bible incidentally, as if we're not sure it really matters. We project Scripture texts on the wall because we believe most people won't have Bibles with them. Why do you suppose people leave their Bibles at home? Isn't it because no one expects that they will carry the Word of God in the door, so the texts are projected? This looks like the old chicken-and-egg routine.

Of course, contemporary culture *is* biblically illiterate. We can't assume that anyone walking into our sanctuaries has the foggiest idea about whether there is a book of Hezekiah in the Old Testament. Nor can we assume that anyone cares about the question. It *is* true that the Bible is ignored, maligned, and misunderstood, but not, one would hope, in church.

I'm convinced that no one is going to be shocked if we crack open a Bible in the building where the church meets. It is the church, after all. Even the seekers won't mind. So go ahead and boldly read the Scriptures in church. No one will be offended, unless offense comes from the gospel itself. Whether the postmodern listener will grant authority to your presentation of the Bible is another matter, but he or she will fight for your right to use your own book.

Just don't bore them with it. That is the sin they might not forgive you for.

If preaching is helping people hear from God, then we're going to have to use the Scriptures, because the Bible is the instrument God uses to make known his will and way. The Bible has authority and if we make it our text, we understand that God will speak powerfully through his Word to change the shape of life and history. As Paul said in 2 Timothy 4:2a, "Preach the word."

The Integrative Model

This book is built upon a model I've come to call *Integrative Preaching*. For too long, the study of homiletics has been built upon a system of polarities (exposition or narrative; explanation or experience), which have forced the preacher into making unproductive choices. My conviction is that preachers shouldn't be forced to choose between preaching the Bible and preaching about "felt needs" of the listeners. Narrative preaching should not be opposed to expository preaching, particularly given that such a vast amount of Scripture is given in story form.

Integration describes the way two distinct entities can come together without compromising integrity. Integrity is about wholeness (like an "integer," or whole number). Integrative preaching, then, is about bringing together things like head and heart; text and today, without sacrificing the integrity of either concern.

It may seem oxymoronic to realize that such mysterious combinations run throughout the Bible. Perhaps the greatest example for preachers is that of the Word become flesh (John 1:14). Jesus didn't choose between divinity and humanity. Preachers, similarly, shouldn't have to choose between the listeners and God's Word.

Integrative Preaching

What's the Big Idea?

Apprehension

Cognitive
Head

What's
what?

Yeah,
but . . .

What's the point?

What's the problem?

Authority

Text —————— Today

Authority

So
what?

Now
what?

What's the story?

What's the differrence?

Heart
Affective

Apprehension

What's the Story? Integrating Text and Heart

The preacher's first task is to engage the listener. Preachers should never assume that the listener comes to church with a deep desire to hear their sermons. People have short attention spans. It's probably more effective for the preacher to imagine the listener sitting with his hands folded saying, "So what? Prove to me that what you're going to say is worth the investment of my time."

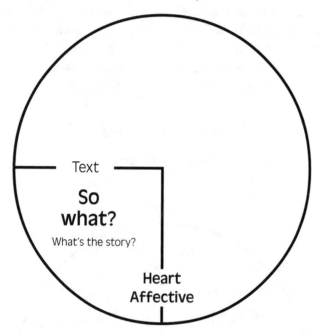

The best way for the preacher to help the listener with their skepticism is to ask the question, "What's the story?" Every text has a story. The Bible is populated with real human beings who are going through almost all of the sorts of things our listeners experience. Working with the humanity who populate the text will give the listeners people with whom they can identify. Perhaps they'll find relevance in the Bible after all.

What's the Point? Integrating Text and Head

The preacher's second task is to teach the listener. People need to know what's what. Identifying with the biblical experience is a good place to start, but usually it isn't enough. Stories tend to be open-ended. Maybe that's why we like them so much—stories allow us to supply our own meanings, but the Bible intends more than that. The Bible has an agenda and preachers are called to proclaim it. We had better speak up and make the truth plain.

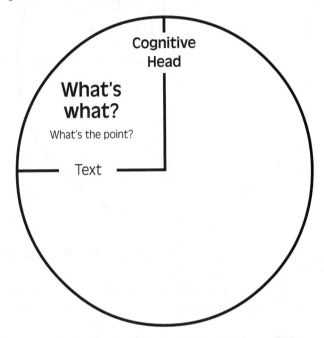

Perhaps the best way for the preacher to achieve this is to answer the question, "What's the point?" of this text. It may or may not be complex or profound, but it's always important, and the listener needs to know it.

What's the Problem? Integrating Head and Today

The preacher's third, and perhaps most compelling task is to help the listener struggle through their natural objections to the text. Just because you've "made your point" doesn't mean anyone's going to respond to it. Our job isn't complete just because the listener understands the point. Imagine, rather, the listener shifting uneasily in his chair, saying, "Yeah, I know what you're saying, but I'm not sure I can (or want to) buy it."

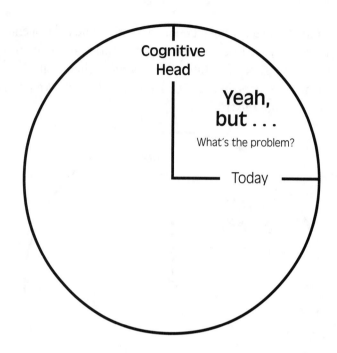

The preacher needs to ask, "What's the problem?" The preacher needs to inquire into the listener's deep-seated objections and assumptions. What obstacle needs to be overcome to get the listener to say, "Yeah, okay, I'm ready to respond"?

What's the Difference? Integrating Today and Heart

The preacher's final operation is to help the listener imagine possibilities that could arise out of obedience to God's call in this sermon. "Now what?" the preacher says. "How will the world change because we've listened to God here this morning?"

This forms the preacher's answer to the question, "What's the difference?" There ought always to be a difference. We should never imagine that our preaching is merely a matter of education or entertainment. We desire to see new things happen by God's grace and for his glory. Just imagine. . . .

Choosing the Text

The first task in preaching is to choose an appropriate text. When students ask me what text they should preach, I tend to answer with ambivalence. "Is it in the Bible?" If so, it's worth preaching. I'm convinced that the Bible is inherently relevant—all of it. Leviticus is worth preaching, as long as we can interpret our text so that listeners in Saskatoon, or listeners in San Francisco—or wherever we might find them—hear the importance and relevance of the Law. My guess is that it would have something to do with the pursuit of holiness and if that isn't relevant today I'm not sure what is.[1]

The central text chosen for Jack's sermon is Hebrews 12:28–29. The earthquake imagery seemed useful to plot development as a metaphor, both for the kingdom and for the instability of human life in contemporary culture. Preachers struggle to offer a sure word in a world that shakes beneath their feet. The relevance of the image to me may have had something to do with the fact that I live near a fault line on the Pacific Coast of the United States.

I developed a similar sermon in 1996 and I have preached versions of it a handful of times since, each time adapting it to fit the challenge of the particular time and culture of the audience. I seldom write a manuscript in full. One of the benefits of that approach is that, if I have cause to preach the sermon again, I'm forced to rebuild it, so it becomes new and fresh.

Here I'll interact with the same basic sermon points more deliberately than I could have in Jack's sermon. Critical sections from the sermon will be given in italics. Commentary will be written in the straight-up font. I'll try to render it as I preached it in my local church, Parkland Fellowship, located in Surrey, British Columbia. I'm fortunate that my pastor and friend, David Horita, himself a fine expositor, doesn't hoard the pulpit, though some in the congregation might wish that he did.

Shaken Foundations—Hebrews 12:28–29

Things Will Get a Little Shaky.

You didn't expect security did you? The Dow is a roller coaster. Your job is redundant. Divorce rates are high enough to make the best of us wonder, and the scientists still warn us of the coming of "the big one." Things will get a little shaky. I priced out earthquake insurance recently. They wanted to charge me an extra 50 percent over the cost of the basic coverage. Can you imagine? It would cost me four hundred dollars for everything else, fire, theft, alien invasion—but if I wanted to be covered against an earthquake, I could pay six hundred dollars, thank you very much.

I decided to take the risk. Of course I squirm a bit every time I read one of those articles in the newspapers or those interviews on television—you know the ones with the seismologists talking about how there's been a major earthquake every fifty years or so in our area. Come to think of it, it's been about fifty years ago since our last big shake.

Like most of us, I'm living with the risk. We all live in the knowledge that this whole thing is unstable, and one good shake could bring it all crashing down around our ears.

I know, you wanted to hear a sermon, not some scattered comments about earthquake preparedness, but I've got to get your ear before you'll listen to me. The quake imagery is direct from the text, as are all good sermonic images. It has that feel of everyday relevance and will forge a useful segue into the meat of the message. If I do my job properly, I'll begin to probe some latent anxiety I know is hiding in the hearts of listeners. I'll work on that again later, but if I can help you feel your insecurity, you'll be more susceptible to the point that's coming.

The people of Israel would have understood. They knew what it was to live with one eye on the seismometer. They had a very long memory and this text takes them all the way back— back to Sinai [Exodus 19] when God spoke on the mountain and the whole earth shook by the sound of his voice. They'd all heard the stories about the smoke and the fire and the God who was not to be messed with. He would speak again, he promised, and this time [it says in v. 26], he'll shake not only the earth but also the heavens.

It's called judgment, and it is coming. The Hebrews knew it, and they expected it. They understood the basic instability of everything created. They knew they were accountable.

There's not a lot of storytelling in the book of Hebrews, but there is a sense of humanity. I'd like to have crafted more of a story out of the few facts I had. I certainly could have created more of a sense of immediacy; however, I was concerned that it could come off sounding contrived. We don't know much about who wrote the letter, and we know little about the specific events that gave rise to it. Here I'm attempting to connect the people listening to me with those who were listening back then. I want my listeners to tap into their own sense of accountability or, at the very least, into their fear that judgment is coming, and that they'll have to give an account. We all have the existential fact of our coming evaluation buried down somewhere inside of us.

> You know it and I know it. Every time the earth moves, we're reminded that there are things we can't control. The world is bigger than we are and, although we don't want to accept it, sometimes we get hit with things so big we just have to deal with them—acts of God we call them [which is a very good thing to call them]. There are forces in this world that can beat us back and throw us down—frightening things when we allow ourselves to think about them. *Things will get a little shaky.*

Notice the repetition of the tagline. This is something I picked up from David Buttrick's book, *Homiletic,* and it makes sense to me.[2] Rather than using obvious point statements that wear people out with their pointedness, I prefer to develop the sermon a little more organically, creating a sense of flow that carries the listener along. There's a structure to the sermon, but I don't need to see the skeleton; I like to keep the bones beneath the skin. Perhaps it helps to think of "plotlining" rather than "outlining."

Still, the listener needs some signposts. I try to use simple, memorable taglines for this purpose. I repeat them two or three times at the beginning and end of each section so the listener can track the flow of my thought. I don't need the listener to memorize my taglines or to write them down on a fill-in-the-blank bulletin insert (not that there's anything wrong with that). I'm satisfied if it happens subliminally.

I like to use taglines that can actually be spoken. Often my students want to use phrases for taglines, instead of speakable sentences. "The Shakiness of Contemporary Life" could be a subheading on a written page, but it makes for a poor tagline. Any preacher who actually tried to say such a thing in his sermon would come off sounding like a professor. Horrors. The last thing I want is for my listeners to think they're at a lecture. It may be bad enough for them that they're listening to a sermon. *"Things will get a little shaky,"* might not be elegant, but at least I can actually say it in the sermon.

I've also found that taglines enable smooth transitions. In this case, it's an easy move from admitting that "things will get a little shaky" to saying that "God's kingdom will never be shaken."

God's Kingdom Will Never Be Shaken.

That's what you need to hear. That's what got me out of bed this morning. I woke up knowing I'd have the opportunity to get up on this platform and tell you this truth that God wants you to know—*His kingdom will survive. It's the one unshakeable thing—the one place where you can get a foothold. When everything else comes crashing down, God's kingdom won't. God's kingdom will never be shaken.*

I love being overt when it comes to the second quadrant of the sermon. I'm trying to make a point, and there's no sense beating around the juniper. This is *not* the time for subtlety. I'll stop the whole thing, if necessary, shake the people by their elbows, and make absolutely sure they know the big idea. My conviction from the study of the text is that the most important idea—the thing God wants them to know from this text at this time—is that he's building a kingdom that will endure. I can't risk them missing this piece, or the sermon is lost.

There are several things we need to notice in this text.

My plan is to walk through the text, itemizing the things that are taught there.

First, verse 26 reminds us that God has shaken the world before, and that he can, no—he will shake it again. The previous shaking refers back to Mount Sinai [vv. 18–21] when God made his presence known on the mountain. That time was so terrifying that the people remembered it to this day.

I didn't feel a need to say too much about Mount Sinai because I'd already described that event in the first quadrant.

Yet, God has promised that he would shake the earth one more time. This is the promise of judgment. It's further described in verse 28 with the use of a second metaphor alongside that of the earthquake—the consuming fire. Both images describe destruction and consumption of the physical elements due to the deliberate intervention of God into the world he has created.

At this point, I could have introduced other texts and information in support of the discussion of God's intent to judge. I decided that for this sermon I wouldn't go much beyond this text.

Second, verse 26 tells us that when, and not if, but when, God shakes the earth again, the effects will extend not only to earth but to the heavens as well.

This indicates that the earthquake of God won't be localized as it was at Sinai. This time it will affect the entire created order.

I've frequently found it helpful to number observations ("first, . . . second, . . . third, . . ."), although these aren't "points" in the traditional rhetorical sense. I'm not giving enough discussion to think of these as propositions. I'm simply laying out the logic of the text in order to support the big idea of the sermon.

Third, verses 27 to 29 indicate that there's one thing that cannot be shaken—the kingdom of God. Though the shaking extends up to heaven, the core of what God has established cannot be touched. Like the consuming fire that burns up everything extraneous to the hard rock core, the earthquake has a purifying function. Everything that's impermanent and unholy will break down and will fall away like so much dust on the ground. The only thing left will be the kingdom God has been building since the beginning of time.

I'll say more about this in a moment. I have an illustration to use, which will take this thought deeper.

Fourth, verse 28 says that all those who are in Christ will find themselves attached to the unshakeable kingdom. We're earthquake-immune. We'll find safety and security in our attachment to God himself in his kingdom.

Again, I feel I want to say more here, but will save some of the motivational language for the fourth quadrant.

Finally, those who are in Christ, who are attached to the unshakeable kingdom, have only one response. That response is worship. That response is service. Actually, the text uses the same word to describe both responses. Some of our English versions have it "worship" and others have it "service," but in fact it's the same thing. We worship in action. We respond through worship.

I don't want to get too caught up in discussion of the Greek. Nevertheless, I've found it interesting and useful to note that the Greek word *latreuō* could be translated either as worship or as service. Just uttering the word *Greek* in a sermon can have a nasty effect on listeners. I prefer to use what I've found in language study without being obvious about it.

In fact, the opening verses of chapter 13 describe what that worship/service might look like: loving our brothers; entertaining strangers; blessing prisoners, even those who've hurt us; staying married; staying satisfied with the good things God has given.

Although I'm trying to stay focused on verse 28, it's helpful to extend the context of the sermon beyond its narrow confines. In this case the list of actions in the opening verses of chapter 13 are an obvious application of the worship/service described in verse 28 of chapter 12.

> We do this because we fear God, which is to say that because we respect him, we have reverence for him. God is holy and can shake the very ground on which we stand. We depend on him for our security and for our future. Thank God we can depend upon his grace.

Now I need to remind them of the primary text.

> Since we are receiving a kingdom *that cannot be shaken* [these last four words need to be spoken with an extra dose of passion] let us give thanks by which we may serve God acceptably, with reverence and awe, for our God is a consuming fire.

Having itemized the logic of the text, it's now time to illustrate.

> I remember visiting Science World a few years ago. A large room had been dedicated to exhibits built from interlocking toy blocks that are sold by the Lego company. Lego blocks have to be one of the greatest toys ever invented, and what these people did with the blocks was incredible. There were full-size racecars and exotic animals, whole cities even—built out of the familiar little plastic blocks. In one corner of the room there was an earthquake simulator where people were encouraged to build a Lego structure on top of a metal plate. Having completed the structure, the builder could push a button, which would cause the plate to shake and vibrate. The object was to test the stability of the structure. Anything loosely connected, all the bits and pieces that weren't strongly supported, would break off and fall away. The idea was to see whether a person could build something strong enough to withstand all the shaking.

That exhibit came to mind when I read verse 27. The passage says that God will shake the earth with the sound of his voice and that everything impermanent, everything unholy, everything extraneous, and everything corrupt will chip off and break away. The shaking will be so severe that everything selfish, and everything that's temporary will crumble and collapse into rubble on the ground. The only thing left standing—the one unshakeable thing—will be the kingdom of God. We'll be saved by our attachment to it.

Enough said!

It's Hard to Find Your Footing When the Ground Is Shaking Underneath.

God's kingdom cannot be shaken. I understand that. At least, I understand it intellectually. And yet, it's hard to find one's footing when the ground is shaking underneath. It's one thing to say that God can make us strong enough to stand the earthquake. My problem is that I don't very much like getting shaken. I like to feel firmness underneath my feet. It's hard to find your footing when the very ground is shaking from below.

This is the third quadrant of the sermon, where we try to engage the problem. I determined that the listener's main objection to this message might be a little more emotional than it is intellectual. If there *is* a God, most of us don't have too much difficulty understanding that a "God" would give his followers strength. Isn't that what he's for? The fact remains, we still don't want to have to go through the trouble. We still don't like the shaking.

In this part of the sermon, we just want to be honest. I try to force myself out of the role of the preacher for a little while. I try to speak for the listener, using the listener's voice. The more authentic this sounds to the listener, the deeper the impact. Ideally, if I can surface the hidden anxieties and issues the listener has locked deep down, God will speak powerfully to the important places in the listener's life.

At times the world seems so stable—so permanent. Other times it feels like everything is moving so quickly and so unpredictably that we're afraid we'll simply fall out of contention. We can't keep up, and yet we can't stop running. At times like this, discussion of God seems so idealistic. It seems so attractive and yet, at the same time, so implausible. You want me to find hope in God and yet God seems so far beyond me. You want me to believe in the promise of God and yet that promise seems such a fairy tale when I'm standing on ground that won't stay still.

Notice how I lined up with the listeners against the preacher. For a moment, the preacher becomes a different presence in the sermon—a presence to react against.

An essay by Joseph Addison, written in about 1710, tells the story of an entrepreneur who finds himself on a desert island. He does a booming business selling a pill that's, "very good against an earthquake."

"Very good against an earthquake"—I think I'd like to get some of those pills. I'm thinking some of you might be interested as well. Maybe we can get a bulk discount. For a pill like that? The market would be endless.

It is unsettling out there. Nothing stays the same for over twenty minutes. Everything changes. I was talking with a group of ministry leaders this week. They agree that it's no longer possible to keep up with the culture. As leaders, we can't possibly have a good understanding of everything that's of interest in the world and everything we're supposed to know. There are so many levels on which we just can't relate. If we can't relate, how can we be relevant? It's depressing.

In the book, Jack Newman takes time to itemize some of the specific issues of the past week that have caused him to lose his footing.

"I've seen my wife in the hospital. I've seen the weakness of good friends. . . ." The more specific the preacher can be, the more authentic the sermon will become for the listener.

Sure, it's comforting to know that God provides me with that firm foundation. Without the handholds on God's kingdom, what do I have? I'd be crumpled in a heap at the bottom of the hill, just like so many others.

Now I want to begin to bring the listener back around. Gently I want to help him or her to move from the "Yeah, but . . ." of the sermon to the, "Yeah, okay." I want them to get from saying, "Yeah, I know what the text says, and I'd like to believe it, but I've got this objection I can't overcome," to the point where they can say, "Yeah, okay, I think I'm ready to respond to what you're saying." In this case I tried to achieve that effect in the original sermon by using an image that would have been familiar to most of my Vancouver area listeners.

Do you know the West Coast Energy building off Georgia Street downtown? It's an amazing building—they say it's earthquake-proof. It features a strong concrete tower, heavily reinforced with steel beams and girders, which is sunk deep into the earth. It's as secure as they could make it.

The building itself, however, is not the tower. No one lives or works in the tower. All the activity occurs in a structure that fits like a sleeve over top of the tower. The sleeve is suspended from the top of the tower by extra large cables. Stabilizer bars have been installed so that in the normal course of events it will feel much like any other building. But if the earth should shake, the people will be secure. Why? *They're attached to the strong tower.* It almost sounds biblical, doesn't it.

Now it's time to finish. The fourth quadrant is the move toward application. I want to imagine the difference this sermon can make in the lives of the listeners, and I want to do it vividly and meaningfully.

We Find Our Footing in the Kingdom of God

In an unstable world where everything is shifting, we can find a sure place to stand in the kingdom of God. Everything else might crumble and everything else may topple, but as long as we're part of the unshakeable kingdom, we'll have a place to stand. We will find our footing.

One of the advantages of this passage is that the text describes a primary way to respond to the sermon. The tricky part is to develop this thinking without getting into a lot of detailed explanation. This isn't the place to be intellectually demanding. This is the point at which we want to motivate response.

Our text gives us two ways to respond to this truth. "Since we're receiving a kingdom that cannot be shaken," the Bible says, *"let us worship God acceptably."* The Greek word could just as easily be translated "serve God." In other words, *let's get busy.* Let's be the people God has called us to be. Let's love one another. Let's worship with our actions. Let's honor the Lord with our lives. We'll stay married. We'll show hospitality to our sisters and to our enemies. We won't covet our neighbor's stuff because we'll be content with the God who promises never to leave us or forsake us [referencing 10:1–6]. This is right and this is fitting. It's an appropriate response to the God before whom we are all accountable—the God who's described as "consuming fire."

In the book, Jack struggles to find some specifics from the lives of his people. He talks about people who are worried about their jobs and others who are struggling to maintain their faith in a postmodern culture. The tone of the appeal is encouraging and motivating. My actual sermon followed the same line.

Some of you have put a lot of faith in your stock portfolios. How's that working out for you? Do you own any Nortel?

During the 1990s technology explosion, Nortel once was the most widely held stock in Canada, and it became notorious for losing almost 80 percent of its value in the technology bust of 2000 to 2002. In front of Canadian congregations, any reference to Nortel still elicits sheepish expressions.

> Others of you are putting confidence in your jobs. But you know there's no greater oxymoron in this part of the country than "job security."

I closed the sermon with another personal story.

A couple of years ago, I was delivering a lecture at First Presbyterian in downtown Seattle. That church had been around for a while. Everything from the thick stone walls to the pictures of the church's former leaders lining those walls spoke of stability and longevity. I spent some time looking into the faces of the people in those pictures—stern, loyal, committed.

In the middle of my lecture, I felt a violent shaking. At first I thought it was a train, but then I realized there were no trains in that part of the downtown core. It was an earthquake! We all looked at one another, unsure of what to do. Should we crawl under the tables? Should we stand in a doorway? I looked at the woman to my right who was confined to a wheelchair. How would I help her if the roof were to fall?

As soon as it had started, the earthquake was over. We looked at each other with relief, and I continued my lecture. Later on, however, I gave the whole thing further thought. If the ground had shaken hard enough, that building could have fallen. Other buildings in the area have. The rocks could have piled in, and all those pictures could have shattered on the ground. That building could have been destroyed, but not what it stands for. The building can fall, but the church cannot. *The kingdom of God can never be destroyed. Hold on to the kingdom. It's your hope and your salvation.*

I always like to find a way for the listeners to respond tangibly to the sermon. Preaching shouldn't be hypothetical. So often our sermons float ideas and propose positions without ever describing a specific expected result. Or if a result is described, it's posed as a hypothetical response to what could happen some day if we ever found ourselves in that situation— one day, maybe, perhaps. It's always about what we'll do some other time when faced with the problem or opportunity the preacher has in mind. It's always about some other time and place later on.

In this case, the expected result of the sermon is given directly in the text. Our response is worship. A creative worship leader will know how to help the listeners respond appropriately to what they've heard.

> We're receiving a kingdom that cannot be shaken. There's only one response, and that response is worship. We must serve God. We must worship him in gratitude for the fact that he has assured our future. We will not be shaken as long as we're attached to the one reliable thing—the kingdom that cannot fall. Though all the earth comes crashing down around our ears, we will not fall. We will not be shaken. We're citizens of the kingdom—the unshakeable kingdom of God.

> Stand with me, all of us together, the physical expression of the kingdom of God in this place. Let us join hands as a symbol of our unity. Let's look into one another's eyes and let us sing together the praises of our God.

It's a token step in some ways, but it is something. Physically connecting the listeners through the joining of hands is a means by which the preacher can help them sense that they're part of something bigger than themselves, something that can't be shaken or destroyed.

I understand that attempting to describe a sermon in printed form is an exercise in futility. I don't expect to be able to replicate the impact for the reader in the pages of a book. A sermon cannot be written any more than it can be published. A sermon is an unrepeatable moment in time when God comes and meets his people in his Word. It's an event in God's presence. It's our passion. It's our calling.

Shaken Foundations

Hebrews 12:28–29

Head

2
God's kingdom will
never be shaken

3
It's hard to find your
footing when the ground
is shaking underneath

Text — Today

1
Things are going to
get a little shaky

4
We find our footing in
the kingdom of God

Heart

6

Only Human

TOWARD AN ANTHROPOLOGY OF PREACHING

Preachers are only human. It seems a shame, given the magnitude of what they attempt. That a human, flawed and finite, could stand in the pulpit and propose to speak for God is a marvel. That God would agree to speak through such humans is a greater mystery yet.

The following serves as a fledgling attempt to grapple with the issues related to the humanity of the preacher. It will deal with the issue around three concerns: The first, under the heading "Immanence," offers a theological basis for preaching. The second, under the heading "Integrity," deals with the weakness of the preacher as a human being. The third, under the heading "Disclosure," asks just how human the preacher can afford to be when preaching. In so doing, I am trying to suggest ways to think about the anthropology or the human aspects of preaching.

That preaching is done by humans is both a pleasure and a puzzler. It is, in the end, the hope of humans everywhere.

Immanence

I've often wondered at the wisdom of preaching. God had other options. That God chose preaching as the means by which he would transmit his will to wayward humans seems foolish when there were so many other possibilities. The significance of the message seems so much more important than what this method seems to indicate.

Express freight companies have made it their business to assure the world that they can be relied upon to deliver any package anywhere, on time and intact. Could preachers make the same promise? It would be hard to imagine a cargo more precious than the gospel of Jesus Christ, yet it would be hard to imagine a delivery system so flawed as the words spoken by the preacher.

There were other options. Why couldn't God have simply transmitted the critical information by a kind of biotechnical cognitive download? He could have simply planted what we need to know in our minds. He could have written it into our DNA.

Of course, in a sense he has. He has written eternity into our hearts. He has created us in his image. Yet still we struggle with the message. Our skulls are thick and our minds too dull to hear the Word that God requires of us. Our tongues are slow to share the truth God wants known.

Everyone who calls on the name of the Lord will be saved. But how can people call on the Lord if they don't believe in the Lord? And how can they believe in the Lord if they've never heard of the Lord? And how can they hear of the Lord if no one has ever told them about the Lord? And how will anyone tell them about the Lord if we don't have any preachers (Rom. 10:12–15)?

Preaching Is What God Does.

Get one thing straight: If preaching is the transmission of divine truth sufficient for women and men to hear from God and respond faithfully to him, then preaching is what God does. No human could effect the kind of spiritual change that preaching intends. Human preachers ought to relieve themselves of that most onerous burden. Instead, such preachers ought to find joy in the fact that they have the opportunity to work as the Lord's instruments in this amazing task.

Preachers need to know their place. Preachers are listeners, the first listeners, perhaps. We've had a head start over everybody else, but we *are* listeners, first and foremost. Understanding that fact gives us greater freedom to be real. The message depends less upon our ability to be God than it does upon our ability to help people hear from God. The relationship between listener and preacher is a peer-level relationship, allowing us freedom to be honest and credible.

I've often been invited to come to churches to "speak." I'm beginning to understand that my purpose in the pulpit is never to speak. My purpose is to listen and to help others listen. It's God who speaks, and the rest of us are there to be humble and to hear. I am not the messenger. No one comes to hear from me. I don't need that kind of pressure. Preaching is what God does.

God Speaks Our Language.

As mysteries go, this is one of the biggest. God is transcendent. "Immortal, invisible, God only wise, in light inaccessible hid from our eyes."[1] The power of worship in this hymn is raised precisely by the fact that we who sing it are quite mortal and visible. It's the "inaccessible" part that bothers us the most. God is wholly Other. Sinless and stainless, he stands above and beyond the mix and the mess of human life.

And yet at the same time, he is with us. Though he is transcendent and above us, he is imminent, which is to say he is present with us. He loved us. He created us, and he's passionate for us. Somehow within the gracious heart of God, he desired to redeem us. But, as Paul said in Romans 10:14, how can we hear the words of salvation without a preacher? We can't receive what we haven't heard, and we can't hear what no one tells us. We needed a preacher, and God provided us with one.

Jesus was the first preacher. Jesus, as God, came down from his glory to live and walk among us. He was the divine Word become flesh (John 1:14; cf. v. 1). Clyde Fant put it well: "The incarnation is the truest theological model for preaching because it was God's ultimate act of communication. Jesus, who was the Christ, most perfectly said God to us because the eternal Word took on human flesh in a contemporary situation. Preaching cannot do otherwise."[2]

Humans Help People Hear from God.

It was our only hope. On their own, humans couldn't hope to find access to God or to speak for God, though we have a long history of trying. One of the earliest and most spectacular examples occurred at Babel, where humans determined to build a stairway to heaven (Genesis 11). Unimpressed, God smashed our tower and squashed our ambition to lift ourselves to his level by straining at our bootstraps. He scattered us and confused our language, thereby complicating the task of the preacher.

It is the vogue to think of postmodernism as something new and fresh when, in fact, its roots are imbedded in soil as old as the events described by Moses in the book of Genesis. One who reads the philosophy of the postmoderns soon discerns that all the hubbub distills to two major problems, cultural and linguistic diversity. Postmodern thinking addresses the reality that we come from different places and speak in different ways. They draw from that the half-truth that we all have our own way of looking at reality. Inasmuch as none of us has finished building our personal towers of divine wisdom, then none of us has a right to give more than our own opinion to anyone else. Proclamation seems arrogant. Our culture does not allow prophetic preaching.

Postmodernism, of course, doesn't take into account the reality that God has every right to preach because he is still in his heaven. If we human instruments rightly understand that God simply is using us to achieve his perfect and eternally wise purposes, then we can speak with confidence. Sure we're flawed and finite. We have sinned and fall short of the glory of God (Rom. 3:23). Yet preachers are called to open our mouths and proclaim the truth anyway. We do so with the understanding that we speak not our own word but the Word of God. Our confidence is not in ourselves but in the God, who speaks through us. It's his project, and we simply have the privilege of participating.

Merrill Unger said it well, "The authority and power, which the inspired oracles possess, become manifest in the pulpit ministry of the faithful expositor of the Bible. He speaks, yet the thrilling fact is true, God at the same time speaks through him."[3]

The postmoderns are right. Humans have no business playing God. That's fine, because we don't intend to. God speaks our language. The Transcendent became immanent, through Jesus Christ, through the inspired Scriptures, and through the Holy Spirit. Humans merely help. We help people hear from God.

Integrity

That God would use a flawed and failing human to communicate his word gives the preacher no license to continue in patterns of depravity. God forbid that we would leave sin unchecked so that grace could abound (Rom. 6:1). Where God is gracious, his people are less so. Listeners have little tolerance for those who preach without integrity.

If there's any doubt as to the truth of this claim, consider the case of the Roman Catholic priesthood. For centuries, the public generally appreciated priests for their spiritual leadership. Now, however, priests are reeling from multiple allegations of gross sexual misconduct. The integrity of the priesthood in general has been damaged, perhaps irreparably. As Donald Cozzens writes, "The absolute confidence once placed in [priests] has faded into a wary cordiality. They have lost their once unquestioned authority, their role as moral leaders and spiritual guides."[4] Once confidence is lost, it's almost impossible to regain. Simply put, character counts.

The Bible Requires Integrity.

Paul's letters to Timothy and Titus provide direct instruction to those aspiring to preach. Paul said preachers must "have a good reputation with outsiders" (1 Tim. 3:7) and must be "worthy of respect" (v. 8). Titus 2:7–8 says the preacher is to set "an example by doing what is good. In your teaching show integrity, seriousness and soundness of speech that cannot be condemned, so that those who oppose you may be ashamed because they have nothing bad to say about us."

This emphasis upon moral integrity runs throughout the Bible, both in the example of people like Job (Job 2:3) and David (1 Kings 9:4; cf. Ps. 78:72), and also in the direct instruction found in the Psalms and Proverbs (for example, Prov. 19:1). Biblically, one gets the idea that it's not sufficient for a preacher to have the gift of the gab. Homiletic skill is not enough. Preaching that honors God and blesses people will be marked by a righteous life.

Etymologically, the word *integrity* describes structural soundness and wholeness. One whose life has integrity is one who can be trusted, who'll tell the truth and who'll live it out. Such a one will practice what he preaches.

The Preacher Requires Grace.

The implication of our need for purity can be frightening to those of us with sufficient integrity to own our spiritual and material infidelities. If we're to have integrity, we first have to be honest with ourselves and honest with God about our weaknesses and failings.

Preaching requires a vital intimacy with God through his Spirit. So what does the preacher do when God seems to go AWOL? How can we preach when the well runs dry? Every preacher vacillates between faith and doubt, hope and fear. It's hard to offer refreshment when you're living in the desert.

Preachers with integrity will also have to admit the limits of their wisdom. Though we love to nurse the "hero-myth," we admit when we're honest that the job is bigger than we are. What do you say that will encourage the abused wife and the abandoned child? How do we proclaim truth to be relevant to people who believe all truth to be relative? What do we do when we lose our joy and our calling feels like drudgery?

Our first response must be to make fact of our failure. There's no point pretending that we're something we're not. Honesty, even about personal weakness, marks a true spiritual leader. The more integrity we have, the greater our willingness to admit our sin. We simply appeal to grace.

Yet, grace feels like such a scandal. We struggle with the idea that someone could get away with so much so easily. When we've been hurt by the sinner's sin, it can be very hard to respond graciously to a leader who has failed us. What do we do with our broken expectations? Consider the case of Bill Clinton. Alan Wolfe of Boston University described the two responses to the former U.S. president's reported sexual misconduct as exemplifying what he called hard and soft Protestantism. Hard Protestants were uncompromising, disciplined, and straight-backboned. Soft Protestants were inclusive, therapeutic, and forgiving.[5] On the one hand we want to "hang 'em high," and on the other hand, we prefer to "give 'em a break." The former approach appeals to the biblical standards of holiness. The latter appeals to the biblical mandate to forgive.

Of course, both of these principles are critical within Scripture. They find their point of integration in the biblical concept of grace. Grace does not relieve people of their responsibility before God's righteous standard. As C. S. Lewis said, "Real forgiveness means looking steadily at the sin, the sin that is left over after all allowances have been made, and seeing it in all its horror, dirt, meanness and malice, and nevertheless being wholly reconciled to the man who did it."[6]

Grace makes no excuses, but then grace makes sure to forgive. That God, for instance, could offer David as an example of integrity (1 Kings 9:4) despite his acts of adultery, murder, and manipulation, is powerfully encouraging.

Preachers understand that they don't offer themselves on the merits of their own character or competency, but on the basis of that which has been granted by Christ. Our ability to preach is entirely a gift of God's grace. We can stand with character intact in his presence only because he has forgiven us. We can lead others competently only because he gifted us. When it comes to it, even those who follow are being gracious to us.

Listeners Require an Example.

Preachers who choose to walk with integrity will provide their message with a measure of authority. The preacher who's not afraid to say, "Do as I say *and* do as I do," walks in a great tradition. Paul himself invited people to join in following his example (Phil. 3:17). If 64 percent of Christian men are struggling with sexual addiction or sexual compulsion, then preachers will need to be models of sexual faithfulness.[7] The one who not only talks truth but also lives truth will preach with power.

The ministry of Billy Graham has provided one of the outstanding contemporary examples of this kind of ethical preaching. Even cynical journalists found Graham to offer a message and an example that were compelling.[8] Clearly, he has been a creative leader. His competency as a leader would not have been sufficient, however, without his character as a man of the Spirit. Early in his ministry, Graham and his team made some hard character choices about the way they'd approach their work. They deliberately determined to avoid even the appearance of financial abuse. They chose to exercise care to avoid the possibility of any perception of sexual impropriety. They agreed to cooperate with any local church that could subscribe to their view of the gospel so as to avoid any sense of competition among churches.

Many may have thought they had taken precautions beyond what was necessary only to fall short somewhere along the way. Yet decades later, Graham's ministry stands as a paragon of ethical propriety. The credibility of his message has been immeasurably enhanced by these commitments to character deliberately chosen and maintained over the years.

Those of us who are committed to the cause of the gospel need to make deliberate choices first to receive God's grace, then to live by it, choosing moment by moment to live in ways that are congruent with our calling. It won't be easy. Sin and humanity go hand in hand. Yet humans who preach require a higher standard. The Bible calls us to be holy as God is holy (1 Peter 1:16). What part of that don't we understand?

Disclosure

I remember a cartoon I read years ago. A pastor and his family are receiving a farewell gift from their congregation. No doubt the pastor had preached faithfully to these people for many years. An elder is presenting him with a very large and heavy looking book, which he's barely able to receive for its sheer weight and bulk. The title of the book is visible on the spine, "The Life and Times of Pastor Smith as Compiled from His Sermon Illustrations, Volume One."

We all know the agony of listening to a preacher who is far too impressed with himself and his own life experiences. Yet few of us would care to listen to a sermon devoid of human experience and real-life color. For his part, the preacher should avoid getting in the way of the message of Scripture. Yet at the same time, the listener finds it desirable if the preacher has a pulse.

How human should a preacher be? How much honest disclosure can preachers afford without causing too much trouble for their listeners?

Our Humanity Gets in the Way.

It's very difficult for even a conscientious preacher to avoid putting a personal spin on the message. The challenge isn't only to understand the text rightly, but to communicate it correctly as well. To achieve this task, the preacher must suspend the insertion of any personal opinions enough to be able to identify what God wants to say. The challenge is to interpret the biblical passage without confusing one's own point of view with that of the Bible.[9] We need to get out of the way of our own sermons.

Preachers who highlight their own person and experience in their preaching run the risk of hindering the objective of the Word of God. Preaching must exalt Christ and Christ alone. The preacher who tells a personal story runs the risk of either looking too good or looking too bad. In the former case, the preacher can appear arrogant and self-serving. In the latter, the preacher risks the negation of either his point or his authority. In both cases, the preacher draws attention to himself at the expense of the text.

Physically, the preacher standing in front of the congregation is the center of attention. The position is seductive. Many preachers succumb to that temptation, encouraging this attention through the way they dress and the way they handle themselves. The response of the congregation can be mesmerizing. When listeners pay more attention to the preacher than to the message being preached, the contract is broken.

Pride is a constant companion. Preachers quickly learn that the pulpit can serve wonderfully as a means of promoting oneself or protecting oneself. The sermon can be intoxicating to preachers looking for ways to advance their personal agendas. Such preachers need to remind themselves that "it's not about me." The sermon does not belong to the preacher.

Truly all do fall short of the glory of God (Rom. 3:23), and the message is borne on feet of clay. Of course, one can cite preachers who are widely praised for their integrity and their blameless character. But for every leader who has kept personal and corporate cleanliness, one can think of a TV preacher or a noted preacher of pop theology who has shown filthy hands in the public spotlight. As Raymond Bailey put it, "We preach the grace of God, yet the preacher who draws from that well too often and too deeply will lack integrity in the eyes of the congregation. Surely, the wise preacher will limit the exposure of personal foibles in order not to tax the listener's sense of forgiveness."[10]

But Humanity Also Helps.

On the other hand, several things can be said in favor of expressing one's humanity in the sermon. One of the difficulties inherent in preaching is the "otherworldliness" of the message. The preacher deals transcendent truth to people who can't escape space and time. How can the finite appreciate the infinite? How can contemporary listeners overcome their subjective natures sufficiently to gain access to the object?[11] Somehow the message has to be perceived as "real." Speaking of the text in "real" terms, offering contemporary examples and tangible human interaction makes the truth more accessible to the listener.

The preacher who accents the human character of the text stands a good chance of at least winning a hearing. The people in the Bible (as well as the original intended audience of the text) are not so removed from the experience of contemporary people. They hurt like we hurt. They felt the same things we feel today. If the preacher can help listeners "*real*-ize" the text, they might be well prepared to at least consider its propositions.

People rely on one another. In a complex, option-laden world, people tend to rely on the advice and recommendations of people they admire or trust. Preachers who are willing to describe their own experience with the text endorse the message of the text. A preacher who has earned the trust of the congregation can greatly enhance the impact of the message through the telling of a few well-chosen personal stories.

Our Humanity Is Inescapable.

At the risk of offending the reader's intelligence, let it be noted that both preacher and listener are inescapably human. In the story, Jack was rightly warned that he could no more renounce his humanity than he can grow gills and swim like a fish. It's simply not possible.

When God created humankind, he deemed his handiwork "good." God understood that when he gave his Word in written form it would require translation and interpretation, inevitably creating confusion as a result. He built emotion and passion into the human experience, knowing full well that these feelings would be difficult to control. Humans are sometimes uncomfortable in their own skin. Men and women misunderstand their own impulses, much less those of one another. It's frustrating, bewildering, and exhilarating. It's part of God's plan.

When Jesus took on flesh and blood (John 1:1–14), he showed the value God places on created human beings. We preach because we have a message. Our humanity would have hindered us from knowing God in his transcendence, except that God was willing to make himself known from within our human experience.

William Placher says, "We can know the transcendent God not as an object within our intellectual grasp but only as a self-revealing subject, and even our knowledge of divine self-revelation must be God's doing."[12] The only way we know anything about God is that he's been gracious enough to make himself known in the world.

Therefore, we preach. God has made himself known in the "down and dirty" of human life. In fact, it's in the deepest of human experiences that God is most fully revealed. The crucifixion of our Lord ought to have taught us that. We should no more find it necessary to divorce our humanity from our preaching than God himself did.

If our experience tells us a disembodied sermon is impossible, and the incarnation tells us it's unnecessary, our listeners will tell us it's unwise. People want to hear about people. One of the faster ways to empty a church is to refuse to tell stories and offer emotion. Jesus himself taught us that one of the most effective ways to offer truth is by encasing it in human narrative. The gospels tell us that "Jesus wept" (John 11:35). When Nathan had to confront David over his sin, he did it with a story (2 Samuel 12). Later, when David went to God to confess his sin, he wrote a heart-wrenching psalm, a deeply emotional expression of his human sorrow for his transgression (Psalm 51).

If the Bible can express such stark human honesty, then why can't a preacher? Preachers must be willing to share their lives with their listeners. They ought to be willing to express their humanity in their preaching. Their listeners will thank them.

Preaching in Human Terms

Preachers love to turn to Paul's second letter to Timothy as a source of motivation: "Preach the Word" (2 Tim. 4:2). We find encouragement in the reminder that all Scripture is given by inspiration of God (3:15–16). Biblical sermons gain authority as they're founded on God's Word.

Yet there's another form of authority in the passage that we often overlook. In the context of a world where evil is on the upswing, Paul encourages Timothy to "continue in what you have learned and have become convinced of," on the basis of two reasons: (1) because "from infancy you have known the holy Scriptures," and (2) "because you know those from whom you have learned it" (2 Tim. 3:14–15).

In Timothy's case, that would have been his mother, Eunice, his grandmother, Lois, and Paul himself. "You . . . know all about my teaching, my way of life, my purpose, faith, patience, love, endurance, persecutions, sufferings" (2 Tim. 3:10). We're quick to appreciate the authority of the Bible in our preaching, and we must. Yet apparently the preacher has authority as well. Paul's human life experience is offered as authority for the credibility of his message.

Preachers need to use the human language. Certainly, we bear our "treasure in jars of clay" (2 Cor. 4:7). We're easily tempted and subtly selfish. We owe everything we have to the grace of God. Therefore we express ourselves humbly and graciously, submitting carefully to the authority of God's Word, even as we offer that Word to others. We who offer ourselves to preach must examine ourselves closely as those called to a higher standard (James 3:1). We don't want to disqualify our message by our actions. We must spurn our pride and live faithfully, if not perfectly, so people will be compelled to listen and respond.

Despite our weakness, God is gracious. He has promised that when we preach the Word it will accomplish its purpose (Isa. 55:11). The Word preached humbly, truthfully, and confidently can be preached with integrity.

Endnotes

Chapter 1: Fault Lines

1. Kenton C. Anderson, *Preaching with Conviction* (Grand Rapids: Kregel, 2001). *Preaching with Integrity* is a sequel to *Preaching with Conviction*, its fictional narrative set approximately one year after the preaching of Jack Newman so convicted city councilman Philip Andrews.
2. Joe E. Trull and James E. Carter, *Ministerial Ethics: Being a Good Minister in a Not-So-Good World* (Nashville: Broadman & Holman, 1993), 80–82.
3. Patrick A. Means, *Men's Secret Wars* (Grand Rapids: Revell, 1999), 132–33.
4. Bill Hybels, "Responsibility to Self," in *Leadership Handbook of Management*, ed. James D. Berkley (Grand Rapids: Baker, 1997), 60–69.

Chapter 2: Footings

1. *The 1995 Grolier Multimedia Encyclopedia*, "earthquakes."
2. The following statistics and reports are taken from Susan Oh, "Terror in Turkey: A Devastating Earthquake Sparks Anger over Relief Efforts," *Macleans*, 30 August 1999, 26–28.
3. Ted Olsen, "Today's Sermon: Thou Shalt Not Steal," *Christianity Today*, 4 February 2002: 13.
4. Charles Bartow, *God's Human Speech* (Grand Rapids: Eerdmans, 1997), 19.

Chapter 3: Frailty

1. Susan Oh, "Terror in Turkey: A Devastating Earthquake Sparks Anger over Relief Efforts," *Macleans*, 30 August 1999, 28.
2. Bryan Chapell, *Christ-Centered Preaching: Redeeming the Expository Sermon* (Grand Rapids: Baker, 1994), 40–44.

Chapter 4: Fidelity

1. Fred Craddock, *Preaching* (Nashville: Abingdon, 1985), 134.
2. Haddon Robinson, *Biblical Preaching: The Development and Delivery of Expository Messages* (Grand Rapids: Baker, 1980), 20.
3. Jonathan Edwards, *A Treatise Concerning Religious Affections in Three Parts*, 1.2.3. Framed in the context of colonial America's First Great Awakening of the 1730s and 1740s, this document has amazing relevance today for its theological and psychological insights.
4. Joseph Addison, *The Tatler*, ed. Donald F. Bond, (London: Oxford, 1993), 240.

Chapter 5: Clinic in Integrative Preaching

1. Rob Bell, "Life in Leviticus," *Leadership*, winter 2002: 45–47.
2. David Buttrick, *Homiletic: Moves and Structures* (Philadelphia: Fortress, 1987), 43–53.

Chapter 6: Only Human

1. Walter Chalmers Smith, "Immortal, Invisible," stanza 1.
2. Clyde E. Fant, *Preaching for Today*, 2d ed. (San Francisco: Harper & Row, 1987), 70.
3. Merrill F. Unger, *Principles of Expository Preaching* (Grand Rapids: Zondervan, 1955), 24.
4. Donald B. Cozzens, "Confronting All of the Priests' Losses," *In Trust*, autumn 2000: 4.
5. Alissa J. Rubin. "Sex Scandal Revives Dilemma over Ethics." www.hotcoco.com (Oct. 4, 1998).
6. C. S. Lewis, *Fern-seed and Elephants and Other Essays on Christianity*, ed. Walter Hooper (Glasgow: Collins, 1975), 42.
7. Patrick A. Means, *Men's Secret Wars* (Grand Rapids: Revell, 1999), 132–33.
8. Billy Graham, *Just As I Am: The Autobiography of Billy Graham* (New York: Zondervan, 1997), 127–29.
9. Walter C. Kaiser Jr., "The Use of Biblical Narrative in Expository Preaching," *The Asbury Seminarian* 34 (July 1979): 14–26.
10. Raymond Bailey, "Ethics in Preaching," in *Handbook of Contemporary Preaching* (Nashville: Broadman, 1992), 549–61.
11. Stanley J. Grenz, *A Primer on Postmodernism* (Grand Rapids: Eerdmans, 1996).
12. William Placher, *The Domestication of Transcendence: How Modern Thinking About God Went Wrong* (Westminster: John Knox, 1996).